What About Him?

Jesus waits for an answer

By Harry S. Carter

March 2017

What About Him?

John 20: 30 – 31

Jesus performed many other signs in the presence of his disciples, which are not recorded in this book. [31] But these are written that you may believe that Jesus is the Messiah, the Son of God, and that by believing you may have life in his name.

Jesus is waiting for an answer

Revelation 3: 20

Here I am! I stand at the door and knock. If anyone hears my voice and opens the door, I will come in and eat with that person, and they with me.

Reflection on Revelation 3:20

"Christ is there standing at the door. He is knocking, where the tense signifies not a perfunctory rap, but a knocking continued in the hope of a response. *If anyone* is an appeal to the individual. Christ promises to enter in to anyone who opens the door."

—Leon Morris from his book *Revelation, p. 83.*

This work is dedicated to the glory of God.

Contents

Introduction

During the time when Brenda and I were members of East Cooper Baptist Church, I had the good fortune of being appointed to the Campus Outreach Board of Directors. In that capacity, I had many interactions with college students and young adults in their 20s and out of college. I also established some relationships with Campus Outreach folks beyond the Charleston area. These experiences were meaningful to me in my growth in the Christian faith.

One conversation I had in this capacity has really stuck with me. I was talking with a college graduate in his mid-twenties about Christianity and I asked him "who was Jesus?" He said he thought He (Jesus) was a great teacher. This young man had grown up in a Christian home in a family with a history of Christianity for generations. I remember being stunned by his response.

That encounter and other such subsequent conversations about Jesus led me to look for biblical explanations of who He is. My formal education is in mathematics and the application of math models to business. So I tend to approach questions from an empirical point of view. To some degree, I have approached this question that way. But I have made a critical adjustment in my approach to faith-based questions. I now come at these questions being convinced that the Bible is the basis of truth.

I have arrived at that position in part based on my experience that the Bible best explains my condition in life and in part based on research about the Bible. But the most important contributor to this approach is faith. I have a strong belief that the Bible is the Word of God. I believe it to be completely accurate in presenting God's truths to us. Certainly, there may be syntax inaccuracies due to translations. Still, I believe that the spiritual truths contained in the Bible are the infallible Word of God.

For this particular work, I will be using the New International Version (NIV) of the Bible unless otherwise noted.

For those who are inclined to look for sources beyond the Bible, I want to point out that there is significant nonbiblical literary evidence for Jesus. Because of my position stated above, I do not elaborate on such an approach. But if you are led to further exploration, I want to identify three excellent sources for your review.

> *Studying the Historical Jesus* by Darrell L. Bock (Baker Academic, 2002)
>
> *Jesus and Christian Origins outside the New Testament* by F. F. Bruce (Eerdmans, 1974)
>
> *A Marginal Jew: Rethinking the Historical Jesus,* vol. 1: *The Roots of the Problem and the Person* by John P. Meier (Doubleday, 1991)

The fundamental purpose of this work is to assist the reader in resolving the question *Who is Jesus?* No other question is more important to us than this one. I am particularly hopeful that the young man who responded, "He is a great teacher" will benefit from this material.

Finally, my prayer for my family and friends is that this work will benefit each one of them in answering this question. My earnest desire in writing this is to leave them something of lasting value. The value is not this work but in what they might find while seeking an answer to the question, *What about Him?*

In the process of this writing, a second critical question occurred to me. While I don't address it in this work, the issue of who is in control is nevertheless worth mentioning. Simply stated,

In my life, am I god or will I let **God** be god?

This question is clearly seen in the comparison of biblical truths to the poem *Invicitus* by William Ernest Henley.

Out of the night that covers me
Black as the Pit from pole to pole,
I thank whatever gods may be
For my unconquerable soul.

In the fell clutch of circumstance
I have not winced nor cried aloud.
Under the bludgeonings of chance
My head is bloody, but unbowed.

Beyond this place of wrath and tears
Looms but the Horror of the shade,
And yet the menace of the years
Finds, and shall find, me unafraid.

It matters not how strait the gate,
How charged with punishments the scroll.
I am the master of my fate:
I am the captain of my soul.

Do you think about this? Do you have an answer to this question about who is in control of your life?

My answer comes from Psalm 119: 33-40.
This is my prayer for me!

Teach me, LORD, the way of your decrees,
that I may follow it to the end.

Give me understanding,
so that I may keep your law
and obey it with all my heart.

Direct me in the path of your commands,
for there I find delight.

Turn my heart toward your statutes
and not toward selfish gain.

Turn my eyes away from worthless things;
preserve my life according to your word.

Fulfill your promise to your servant,
so that you may be feared.

Take away the disgrace I dread,
for your laws are good.
How I long for your precepts!
In your righteousness preserve my life.

I want to acknowledge those who have meant so much to me in this journey of faith and understandings. So, my heartfelt thanks go out to all of those listed here.

The current and former pastors of First United Methodist Church Statesboro Georgia

The current and former pastors, elders and deacons of East Cooper Baptist Church Charleston SC

The pastors and deacons of First Baptist Church of Charleston SC

All those other saints whose teaching and writing have shaped my understanding about God

I mention a few specifically by name because of their unique influence:

Don Adams
Carter Berkley
Marshall Blalock
Andy Boyer
Buster Brown
Dave Bruner
Elick and Margaret Bullington
Kenny Caldwell
Hugh Davis
Dave Golden
John Graham
John Grinalds
Bill Hatcher
Dean Henderson

Dan Legare
Steve Lindenmeyer
Patricia McArver (editorial advisor)
Robert McCants
Frank and Lisa Morris
Rick Mosteller
Gilbert Ramsey
Josh Romine
J. Robert Smith
Claude Tackett
Carrie and Ed Timmerman

Finally, the support and love of family members has been enabling and inspirational.

Bill & Carol Carter	Parents
Brenda	Wife
Ashley	Daughter
Bill & Erica	Son and Daughter-in-law
Lauren, Lindsey & Courtney	Grandchildren
Grandparents, aunts and uncles, cousins and our extended families	

What About Him?

Introduction

A basic question for all of us...Christians and non-Christians alike . . . is the following: What do we believe about Jesus Christ?

Whether we like it or not, Christ is a central figure in all of history. Many factors provide evidence for this conclusion such as the impact his life has had on our calendar, the number of bibles printed and in circulation compared to other books, the number of people who profess to believe in Him, and the congruence of Christianity with history.

This work is simply an account of how I have answered this question. I hope that my effort will encourage you, the reader, to reflect deeply about your beliefs about Jesus Christ. Resolve it for yourself. This question ... What about Him? ... is fundamental to life!

The amount of work written on this question is really beyond enumeration. So we could become overwhelmed by an endless examination of "foolish controversies" and "rabbit trails" as we attempt to address the basic question of what we believe about Jesus Christ. But let's avoid that and heed the advice of theologian Charles Spurgeon.

Charles H. Spurgeon was born in Essex England in 1834 and died in 1892. He was pastor of the New Park Street Chapel in London for 38 years. A prolific writer, he was prominent in the Reformed Baptist tradition movement. There is a website devoted to his compendium of daily devotionals. One of his works is a daily devotional entitled *Morning and Evening* (December 1, 2001). From this work I have selected his morning devotion for November 19 which cites the following text from Titus Chapter 3.

> "⁹ But avoid foolish controversies and genealogies and arguments and quarrels about the law, because these are unprofitable and useless."

While it would be easy to get bogged down in addressing our topic, Spurgeon suggests setting aside the academic arguments to focus on basic questions including the following:

Do I believe in Jesus Christ?

To believe (or not), I must first resolve for myself who He is. So my basic question — What about Him? — follows from that November 19th devotional. Public debate about Christ and the Bible will continue to be with us; but each individual must answer this fundamental question of life. Ignoring the question is certainly one answer . . . but it is a dangerous one!

A systematic inquiry
My approach is to consider the 3 – 5 basic questions we often ask when examining such an issue:

Who?
What?
Why?
How?
So what?

As I attempt to answer these questions, I want to be clear about methodology. My source for answering these questions is the Bible. Over the years, I have come to believe in the truth of the Bible. I accept it as the word of God and therefore without error. Consequently, I do not have the option to accept selected portions of the Bible while rejecting others. Likewise, I do not have the authority to interpret the Bible to conform to my own opinions on a matter.

I make every effort to be conservative in my approach of using the Bible to answer questions such as those posed in this work. I fully recognize that some may disagree with this approach. But please give it a chance!

Josh McDowell did.

Josh thought Christianity was a joke. But he took seriously the challenge from a group of new friends who were Christians and who convinced him to make a "rigorous, intellectual examination of the claims of Jesus Christ." He reports the following.

> I took the challenge seriously. I spent months in research. I even dropped out of school for a time to study in the historically rich libraries of Europe. I found evidence in abundance. I had to admit that the Old and New Testament documents were some of the most reliable writings of antiquity.
>
> *This account is taken from his book, More Than a Carpenter*
> *by Josh and Sean McDowell.*

In this work, I will attempt to address three basic questions:

Who is Jesus?

What did He do and why?

What does this mean for me?

I am not capable of producing original work in this area. I consider myself a student with much still to learn. Therefore, I am heavily dependent on the works and teachings of others. In the Appendix, you will find a list of those books which have significantly influenced my thinking on questions of faith.

In addition, I must acknowledge the teachings of John Piper, retired pastor of Bethlehem Baptist Church in Minneapolis, Minnesota. I specifically encourage you to listen to his sermon series entitled the "Person of Christ." These and many other sermons are available at the Desiring God website (www.desiringgod.com).

Chapter 1
Who Is Jesus Christ?

As I examined this question, I approached it from several points of view cited in the Bible.

God – what did He say about Jesus?

Old Testament prophecies about Jesus.

The angel Gabriel spoke to Mary about Jesus.

John the Baptist spoke about His coming.

John (the apostle) wrote about what he heard and saw concerning Jesus.

Peter wrote about what he heard and saw concerning Jesus.

Thomas wrote about what he heard and saw concerning Jesus.

Luke wrote about what he heard and saw concerning Jesus.

Paul wrote about his encounter with Jesus (Damascus Road).

Author of Hebrews wrote about Jesus.

Jesus made a number of claims about Himself.

Before we begin answering this question using texts from the Bible, let's review a few of the most common answers to the question, "Who is Jesus Christ?"

King of the Jews
The Jewish nation was looking for a king to deliver them from the hardships of Roman rule and law. They wanted a king like David or Solomon to rescue them and restore Israel to "most favored nation status." They were looking forward to a powerful ruler.

Carpenter
By trade, Jesus was a carpenter...not very high in the socio-economic order in that day. So is that our best conclusion of who He is as a central figure in history?

Teacher
He taught in the synagogues using the Old Testament law...the writings of Moses . . . and He taught using His own parables. Beginning at age 12, He was highly regarded for His knowledge of the Scripture and His wisdom in teaching. Is *teacher* the best description of Him?

Magician
He performed a number "miracles" which resulted in large crowds following Him. So was He a magician?

Madman
He made a number of outlandish claims to include "destroy this temple and I will raise it up in three days." Does that mean He was deranged?

A "great man"

If we combine His teachings with the way He helped people, can we conclude that He was one of the great men of history?

Myth

Could Jesus have been a mythological figure who never really existed?

God's Answer

Let's begin to answer the question by examining what God said about Jesus as recorded in Matthew.

In Matthew 3, we find the following.

> [16] As soon as Jesus was baptized, he went up out of the water. At that moment heaven was opened, and he saw the Spirit of God descending like a dove and alighting on him. [17] And a voice from heaven said, **"This is my Son, whom I love; with him I am well pleased."**

In Matthew 17, we find the following.

> [5] While he was still speaking, a bright cloud covered them, and a voice from the cloud said, **"This is my Son, whom I love; with him I am well pleased. Listen to him!."**

So we have God indicating that Jesus is His Son and He is well pleased with Him. We could stop here and have the answer to the first question. But it is worthwhile to continue this examination. So I now turn to the Old Testament for five selected prophecies about Jesus.

Old Testament

From Isaiah Chapter 7, we find the following.

¹⁴ Therefore the Lord himself will give you a sign: The virgin will conceive and give birth to a son, and will call him Immanuel.

The entire chapter from Isaiah 53 is relevant.

Who has believed our message
and to whom has the arm of the LORD been revealed?
² He grew up before him like a tender shoot,
and like a root out of dry ground.
He had no beauty or majesty to attract us to him,
nothing in his appearance that we should desire him.

³ He was despised and rejected by mankind,
a man of suffering, and familiar with pain.
Like one from whom people hide their faces
he was despised, and we held him in low esteem.

⁴ Surely he took up our pain
and bore our suffering,
yet we considered him punished by God,
stricken by him, and afflicted.
⁵ But he was pierced for our transgressions,
he was crushed for our iniquities;
the punishment that brought us peace was on him,
and by his wounds we are healed.

⁶ We all, like sheep, have gone astray,
each of us has turned to our own way;
and the LORD has laid on him
the iniquity of us all.

⁷ He was oppressed and afflicted,
  yet he did not open his mouth;
he was led like a lamb to the slaughter,
  and as a sheep before its shearers is silent,
  so he did not open his mouth.
⁸ By oppression and judgment he was taken away.
  Yet who of his generation protested?
For he was cut off from the land of the living;
  for the transgression of my people he was punished.

⁹ He was assigned a grave with the wicked,
  and with the rich in his death,
though he had done no violence,
  nor was any deceit in his mouth.

¹⁰ Yet it was the LORD's will to crush him and
cause him to suffer,
  and though the LORD makes his life an offering for sin,
he will see his offspring and prolong his days,
  and the will of the LORD will prosper in his hand.

¹¹ After he has suffered,
  he will see the light of life and be satisfied;
by his knowledge my righteous servant will justify many,
  and he will bear their iniquities.
¹² Therefore I will give him a portion among the great,
  and he will divide the spoils with the strong,
because he poured out his life unto death,
  and was numbered with the transgressors.
For he bore the sin of many,
  and made intercession for the transgressors.

Zechariah 9 is a prediction of His entrance into Jerusalem.

> 9 Rejoice greatly, Daughter Zion!
>   Shout, Daughter Jerusalem!
> **See, your king comes to you,**
>   **righteous and victorious,**
> **lowly and riding on a donkey,**
>   **on a colt, the foal of a donkey.**

Psalm 22 foretells how the soldiers would dispose of His garments when He was crucified.

> 16 Dogs surround me,
>   a pack of villains encircles me;
>   they pierce my hands and my feet.
> 17 All my bones are on display;
>   people stare and gloat over me.
> **18 They divide my clothes among them**
>   **and cast lots for my garment.**

Psalm 2 also indicates Jesus as God's Son.

> 7 I will proclaim the LORD's decree:
>
> **He said to me, "You are my son;**
>   **today I have become your father.**

Now we turn our attention to New Testament recordings which address our first question, "Who is He?"

New Testament

In Luke 1 we find the following account of what the angel said to Mary regarding Jesus.

26 In the sixth month of Elizabeth's pregnancy, God sent the angel Gabriel to Nazareth, a town in Galilee, 27 to a virgin pledged to be married to a man named Joseph, a descendant of David. The virgin's name was Mary. 28 The angel went to her and said, "Greetings, you who are highly favored! The Lord is with you."

29 Mary was greatly troubled at his words and wondered what kind of greeting this might be. 30 But the angel said to her, "Do not be afraid, Mary; you have found favor with God. 31 You will conceive and give birth to a son, and you are to call him Jesus. 32 He will be great and will be called the Son of the Most High. The Lord God will give him the throne of his father David, 33 and he will reign over Jacob's descendants forever; his kingdom will never end."

34 "How will this be," Mary asked the angel, "since I am a virgin?"

35 The angel answered, "The Holy Spirit will come on you, and the power of the Most High will overshadow you. **So the holy one to be born will be called the Son of God.**

Based on this account, Jesus Christ is the Son of God.

What does John the Baptist have to say about this question? We find the following in John Chapter 1 (ESV).

29 The next day he saw Jesus coming toward him, and said, "Behold, the Lamb of God, who takes away the sin of the world! 30 This is he of whom I said, 'After me comes a man who ranks before me, because he was before me.'

³¹ I myself did not know him, but for this purpose I came baptizing with water, that he might be revealed to Israel." ³² And John bore witness: "I saw the Spirit descend from heaven like a dove, and it remained on him. ³³ I myself did not know him, but he who sent me to baptize with water said to me, 'He on whom you see the Spirit descend and remain, this is he who baptizes with the Holy Spirit.' ³⁴ **And I have seen and have borne witness that this is the Son of God."**

So John the Baptist testifies to the same thing...Jesus Christ is the Son of God.

Jesus put this question directly to His twelve disciples. We find the answer coming from Peter in Matthew Chapter 16 as follows.

¹³ Now when Jesus came into the district of Caesarea Philippi, he asked his disciples, "Who do people say that the Son of Man is?" ¹⁴ And they said, "Some say John the Baptist, others say Elijah, and others Jeremiah or one of the prophets."

¹⁵ **He said to them, "But who do you say that I am?"** ¹⁶ **Simon Peter replied, "You are the Christ, the Son of the living God."** ¹⁷ And Jesus answered him, "Blessed are you, Simon Bar-Jonah! For flesh and blood has not revealed this to you, but my Father who is in heaven.

¹⁸ And I tell you, you are Peter, and on this rock I will build my church, and the gates of hell shall not prevail against it. ¹⁹ I will give you the keys of the kingdom of heaven, and whatever you bind on earth shall be bound in heaven, and whatever you loose on earth shall be loosed in heaven." ²⁰ Then he strictly charged the disciples to tell no one that he was the Christ.

Here we have Peter responding in the same manner and Jesus attributing Peter's ability to answer correctly as inspired by God!

In John Chapter 1, we find the following account of Nathanael's statement regarding the identity of Jesus.

43 The next day Jesus decided to leave for Galilee. Finding Philip, he said to him, "Follow me."

44 Philip, like Andrew and Peter, was from the town of Bethsaida. 45 Philip found Nathanael and told him, "We have found the one Moses wrote about in the Law, and about whom the prophets also wrote—Jesus of Nazareth, the son of Joseph."

46 "Nazareth! Can anything good come from there?" Nathanael asked.

"Come and see," said Philip.

47 When Jesus saw Nathanael approaching, he said of him, "Here truly is an Israelite in whom there is no deceit."

48 "How do you know me?" Nathanael asked.

Jesus answered, "I saw you while you were still under the fig tree before Philip called you."

49 Then Nathanael declared, "Rabbi, you are the Son of God; you are the king of Israel."

In John Chapter 20, we find Jesus helping Thomas believe that He has risen. When Thomas is able to actually touch Him, he exclaims, "My Lord and my God."

24 Now Thomas (also known as Didymus), one of the Twelve, was not with the disciples when Jesus came. 25 So the other disciples told him, "We have seen the Lord!"

But he said to them, "Unless I see the nail marks in his hands and put my finger where the nails were, and put my hand into his side, I will not believe."

26 A week later his disciples were in the house again, and Thomas was with them. Though the doors were locked, Jesus came and stood among them and said, "Peace be with you!" 27 Then he said to Thomas, "Put your finger here; see my hands. Reach out your hand and put it into my side. Stop doubting and believe."

28 **Thomas said to him, "My Lord and my God!"**

29 Then Jesus told him, "Because you have seen me, you have believed; blessed are those who have not seen and yet have believed."

In this same chapter in John, the apostle and author of this gospel, writes the following.

30 Jesus performed many other signs in the presence of his disciples, which are not recorded in this book. 31 **But these are written that you may believe that Jesus is the Messiah, the Son of God**, and that by believing you may have life in his name.

Paul comes to this same conclusion as he writes the following in Romans Chapter 1.

1 Paul, a servant of Christ Jesus, called to be an apostle and set apart for the gospel of God — 2 the gospel he promised beforehand through his prophets in the Holy Scriptures 3 regarding his Son, who as to his earthly life was a descendant of David, 4 **and who through the Spirit of holiness was appointed the Son of God in power by his resurrection from the dead: Jesus Christ our Lord.** 5 Through him we received grace and apostleship to call all

the Gentiles to the obedience that comes from faith for his name's sake.

Finally, we find the following from the New Testament writer of Hebrews in Chapter 1.

In the past God spoke to our ancestors through the prophets at many times and in various ways, 2 but in these last days he has spoken to us by his Son, whom he appointed heir of all things, and through whom also he made the universe. 3 The Son is the radiance of God's glory and the exact representation of his being, sustaining all things by his powerful word. After he had provided purification for sins, he sat down at the right hand of the Majesty in heaven.

4 So he became as much superior to the angels as the name he has inherited is superior to theirs. 5 For to which of the angels did God ever say,

> **"You are my Son;
> today I have become your Father"?**

Jesus' Claims about Himself

In this section we will look at eight claims Jesus made about Himself. As we examine each passage, look for the common theme running through these claims.

1. Son of God

In John Chapter 3, Jesus said this about His coming.

9 "How can this be?" Nicodemus asked.

10 "You are Israel's teacher," said Jesus, "and do you not understand these things? 11 Very truly I tell you, we speak

of what we know, and we testify to what we have seen, but still you people do not accept our testimony.

¹² I have spoken to you of earthly things and you do not believe; how then will you believe if I speak of heavenly things? ¹³ No one has ever gone into heaven except the one who came from heaven — the Son of Man. ¹⁴ Just as Moses lifted up the snake in the wilderness, so the Son of Man must be lifted up, ¹⁵ that everyone who believes may have eternal life in him."

¹⁶ For God so loved the world that he gave his one and only Son, that whoever believes in him shall not perish but have eternal life. ¹⁷ For God did not send his Son into the world to condemn the world, but to save the world through him. ¹⁸ Whoever believes in him is not condemned, but whoever does not believe stands condemned already because they have not believed in the name of God's one and only Son.

¹⁹ This is the verdict: Light has come into the world, but people loved darkness instead of light because their deeds were evil. ²⁰ Everyone who does evil hates the light, and will not come into the light for fear that their deeds will be exposed. ²¹ But whoever lives by the truth comes into the light, so that it may be seen plainly that what they have done has been done in the sight of God.

2. One with God

In John 8 and 17, we find the following claims by Jesus.

John 8

⁵⁴ Jesus replied, "If I glorify myself, my glory means nothing. My Father, whom you claim as your God, is the one who glorifies me. ⁵⁵ Though you do not know him, I

know him. If I said I did not, I would be a liar like you, but I do know him and obey his word. 56 Your father Abraham rejoiced at the thought of seeing my day; he saw it and was glad."57 "You are not yet fifty years old," they said to him, "and you have seen Abraham!"

58 "Very truly I tell you," **Jesus answered, "before Abraham was born, I am!"** 59 At this, they picked up stones to stone him, but Jesus hid himself, slipping away from the temple grounds.

There are two critical points in this passage. First, Jesus indicates that He existed before Abraham. Second, He refers to Himself as "I Am." This same phrase appears in Exodus 3:14.

14 God said to Moses, "**I am** who **I am**. This is what you are to say to the Israelites: '**I am** has sent me to you.'"

Jesus is clearly claiming that He and God are one.

In the high priestly prayer in this chapter, Jesus repeats this claim in John 17: 20-23.

20 "My prayer is not for them alone. I pray also for those who will believe in me through their message, 21 that all of them may be one, **Father, just as you are in me and I am in you.** May they also be in us so that the world may believe that you have sent me.

22 I have given them the glory that you gave me, **that they may be one as we are one—** 23 I in them and you in me—so that they may be brought to complete unity. Then the world will know that you sent me and have loved them even as you have loved me.

3. Messiah (king from the line of David to save Israel)

In John Chapter 4, we find Jesus' claim that He is the Messiah as follows.

> [19] "Sir," the woman said, "I can see that you are a prophet. [20] Our ancestors worshiped on this mountain, but you Jews claim that the place where we must worship is in Jerusalem."
>
> [21] "Woman," Jesus replied, "believe me, a time is coming when you will worship the Father neither on this mountain nor in Jerusalem. [22] You Samaritans worship what you do not know; we worship what we do know, for salvation is from the Jews. [23] Yet a time is coming and has now come when the true worshipers will worship the Father in the Spirit and in truth, for they are the kind of worshipers the Father seeks. [24] God is spirit, and his worshipers must worship in the Spirit and in truth."
>
> **[25] The woman said, "I know that Messiah" (called Christ) "is coming. When he comes, he will explain everything to us."**
>
> **[26] Then Jesus declared, "I, the one speaking to you — I am he."**

4. Bread of Life

John Chapter 6 is heavily focused on the topic of bread. In the following verses we find Jesus' claim that He is the "bread of life."

> [25] When they found him on the other side of the lake, they asked him, "Rabbi, when did you get here?"
>
> [26] Jesus answered, "Very truly I tell you, you are looking for me, not because you saw the signs I performed but because

you ate the loaves and had your fill. ²⁷ Do not work for food that spoils, but for food that endures to eternal life, which the Son of Man will give you. For on him God the Father has placed his seal of approval."

²⁸ Then they asked him, "What must we do to do the works God requires?"

²⁹ Jesus answered, "The work of God is this: to believe in the one he has sent."

³⁰ So they asked him, "What sign then will you give that we may see it and believe you? What will you do? ³¹ Our ancestors ate the manna in the wilderness; as it is written: 'He gave them bread from heaven to eat.' "

³² Jesus said to them, "Very truly I tell you, it is not Moses who has given you the bread from heaven, but it is my Father who gives you the true bread from heaven. ³³ For the bread of God is the bread that comes down from heaven and gives life to the world."

³⁴ "Sir," they said, "always give us this bread."

³⁵ Then Jesus declared, "I am the bread of life. Whoever comes to me will never go hungry, and whoever believes in me will never be thirsty. ³⁶ But as I told you, you have seen me and still you do not believe.

³⁷ All those the Father gives me will come to me, and whoever comes to me I will never drive away. ³⁸ For I have come down from heaven not to do my will but to do the will of him who sent me. ³⁹ And this is the will of him who sent me, that I shall lose none of all those he has given me, but raise them up at the last day. ⁴⁰ For my Father's will is that everyone who looks to the Son and believes in him shall have eternal life, and I will raise them up at the last day."

I see four major points in this passage.

- The "work" God requires of us is to Believe in Him (verses 28-29).

- Those who do will Come to Him (verse 37a).

- Those who come will be Kept by Him (verse 37b).

- Those who are kept will be Raised by Him (verses 39b-40).

Jesus continued to teach them; but many just did not get it...as we see from the following passage.

> [43] "Stop grumbling among yourselves," Jesus answered. [44] "No one can come to me unless the Father who sent me draws them, and I will raise them up at the last day. [45] It is written in the Prophets: 'They will all be taught by God.' Everyone who has heard the Father and learned from him comes to me. [46] No one has seen the Father except the one who is from God; only he has seen the Father.
>
> [47] Very truly I tell you, the one who believes has eternal life. [48] I am the bread of life. [49] Your ancestors ate the manna in the wilderness, yet they died. [50] But here is the bread that comes down from heaven, which anyone may eat and not die. [51] **I am the living bread that came down from heaven. Whoever eats this bread will live forever. This bread is my flesh, which I will give for the life of the world."**

Isaiah prophesied about this in Chapter 55 as follows.

> "Come, all you who are thirsty,
>   come to the waters;
> and you who have no money,
>   come, buy and eat!

Come, buy wine and milk
    without money and without cost.
² **Why spend money on what is not bread,**
    and your labor on what does not satisfy?
Listen, listen to me, and eat what is good,
    and you will delight in the richest of fare.
³ Give ear and come to me;
    listen, that you may live.
I will make an everlasting covenant with you,
    my faithful love promised to David.
⁴ See, I have made him a witness to the peoples,
    a ruler and commander of the peoples.
⁵ Surely you will summon nations you know not,
    and nations you do not know will come running to you,
because of the LORD your God,
    the Holy One of Israel,
    for he has endowed you with splendor."

5. Light of the World

Jesus indicates that He is the light that has come into the world in Chapter 3 of John as follows.

¹⁹ This is the verdict: **Light has come into the world,** but people loved darkness instead of light because their deeds were evil. ²⁰ Everyone who does evil hates the light, and will not come into the light for fear that their deeds will be exposed. ²¹ But whoever lives by the truth comes into the light, so that it may be seen plainly that what they have done has been done in the sight of God.

In John Chapter 8, He refers to Himself as "the light of the world."

¹² When Jesus spoke again to the people, he said, "I am the light of the world. Whoever follows me will never walk in darkness, but will have the light of life."

Also, He uses similar language in John Chapter 9.

⁵ While I am in the world, I am the light of the world."

6. Gate/Door and Shepherd

In John 10, Jesus indicates that He is the door for His sheep. We need to look back at Isaiah 53 and be reminded of the prophet's use of the phrase "all we like sheep have gone astray."

"Very truly I tell you Pharisees, anyone who does not enter the sheep pen by the gate, but climbs in by some other way, is a thief and a robber. ² The one who enters by the gate is the shepherd of the sheep. ³ The gatekeeper opens the gate for him, and the sheep listen to his voice. He calls his own sheep by name and leads them out. ⁴ When he has brought out all his own, he goes on ahead of them, and his sheep follow him because they know his voice. ⁵ But they will never follow a stranger; in fact, they will run away from him because they do not recognize a stranger's voice." ⁶ Jesus used this figure of speech, but the Pharisees did not understand what he was telling them.

⁷ Therefore Jesus said again, **"Very truly I tell you, I am the gate for the sheep**. ⁸ All who have come before me are thieves and robbers, but the sheep have not listened to them. ⁹ I am the gate; whoever enters through me will be saved.** They will come in and go out, and find pasture. ¹⁰ The thief comes only to steal and kill and destroy; I have come that they may have life, and have it to the full.

[11] "I am the good shepherd. The good shepherd lays down his life for the sheep. [12] The hired hand is not the shepherd and does not own the sheep. So when he sees the wolf coming, he abandons the sheep and runs away. Then the wolf attacks the flock and scatters it. [13] The man runs away because he is a hired hand and cares nothing for the sheep.

[14] "I am the good shepherd; I know my sheep and my sheep know me — [15] just as the Father knows me and I know the Father — and I lay down my life for the sheep. [16] I have other sheep that are not of this sheep pen. I must bring them also. They too will listen to my voice, and there shall be one flock and one shepherd. [17] The reason my Father loves me is that I lay down my life — only to take it up again. [18] No one takes it from me, but I lay it down of my own accord. I have authority to lay it down and authority to take it up again. This command I received from my Father."

In this previous passage, we also find Jesus claiming to be the good shepherd. He establishes one flock. He indicates that they (some sheep) are not of the same pen. Again, He refers to God as His father and that He received this command from God.

7. The Vine

In John Chapter 15, Jesus presents this claim.

"I am the true vine, and my Father is the gardener. [2] He cuts off every branch in me that bears no fruit, while every branch that does bear fruit he prunes so that it will be even more fruitful. [3] You are already clean because of the word I have spoken to you. [4] Remain in me, as I also remain in you. No branch can bear fruit by itself; it must remain in the vine. Neither can you bear fruit unless you remain in me.

⁵ "I am the vine; you are the branches. If you remain in me and I in you, you will bear much fruit; apart from me you can do nothing. ⁶ If you do not remain in me, you are like a branch that is thrown away and withers; such branches are picked up, thrown into the fire and burned. ⁷ If you remain in me and my words remain in you, ask whatever you wish, and it will be done for you. ⁸ This is to my Father's glory, that you bear much fruit, showing yourselves to be my disciples.

Jesus claims that He is the source of my ability to bear fruit and apart from Him I can do nothing of spiritual significance. He also indicates a very disturbing outcome for me if I do not remain in Him.

8. The Way, the Truth, and the Life
In John 14, Thomas is confused and asks Jesus how they will know the way to where He is going. Jesus responds in the following passage.

⁵ Thomas said to him, "Lord, we don't know where you are going, so how can we know the way?"

⁶ **Jesus answered, "I am the way and the truth and the life. No one comes to the Father except through me.** ⁷ If you really know me, you will know my Father as well. From now on, you do know him and have seen him."

⁸ Philip said, "Lord, show us the Father and that will be enough for us."

⁹ Jesus answered: "Don't you know me, Philip, even after I have been among you such a long time? **Anyone who has seen me has seen the Father. How can you say, 'Show us the Father'?** ¹⁰ **Don't you believe that I am in the Father, and that the Father is in me?** The words I say to you I do

not speak on my own authority. Rather, it is the Father, living in me, who is doing his work.

[11] Believe me when I say that I am in the Father and the Father is in me; or at least believe on the evidence of the works themselves. [12] Very truly I tell you, whoever believes in me will do the works I have been doing, and they will do even greater things than these, because I am going to the Father.

Jesus also reaffirms His claim that He and the Father are one in this passage.

Summary

In the passages we studied above, we find the following multiple claims made by Jesus about who He is.

1. Son of God

2. One with God

3. Messiah

4. Bread of Life

5. Light of the World

6. Gate/Door and Shepherd

7. The Vine

8. The Way (to God), the Truth, and the Life

What common theme did you observe? For me, the common theme is His deity...He is of God! Why do you think the Bible presents Jesus in so many different ways?

In the next chapter, we will examine what Jesus did and why.

Chapter 2
What Did He Do and Why?

In this chapter, we will examine five major activities of Jesus.

1. He Prayed

2. He Built a Team

3. He Taught

4. He Performed Miracles (signs)

5. He Sacrificed (Obeyed His Father)

He Prayed

Jesus taught us how to pray in Matthew Chapter 6. The Lord's Prayer has become one of the most familiar passages in the history of mankind.

> [5]And when you pray, do not be like the hypocrites, for they love to pray standing in the synagogues and on the street corners to be seen by others. Truly I tell you, they have received their reward in full. **[6] But when you pray, go into your room, close the door and pray to your Father, who is unseen. Then your Father, who sees what is done in secret, will reward you. [7] And when you pray, do not keep on babbling like pagans, for they think they will be heard because of their many words.** [8] Do not be like them, for your Father knows what you need before you ask him.
>
> [9] **"This, then, is how you should pray:**

"'Our Father in heaven,
hallowed be your name,
¹⁰ your kingdom come,
your will be done,
   on earth as it is in heaven.
¹¹ Give us today our daily bread.
¹² And forgive us our debts,
   as we also have forgiven our debtors.
¹³ And lead us not into temptation,
   but deliver us from the evil one.'

¹⁴ For if you forgive other people when they sin against you, your heavenly Father will also forgive you. ¹⁵ But if you do not forgive others their sins, your Father will not forgive your sins.

He followed the discipline of prayer as recorded in Luke Chapter 6.

¹² **One of those days Jesus went out to a mountainside to pray, and spent the night praying to God.** ¹³ When morning came, he called his disciples to him and chose twelve of them, whom he also designated apostles: ¹⁴ Simon (whom he named Peter), his brother Andrew, James, John, Philip, Bartholomew, ¹⁵ Matthew, Thomas, James son of Alphaeus, Simon who was called the Zealot, ¹⁶ Judas son of James, and Judas Iscariot, who became a traitor.

He prayed for Peter in Luke Chapter 22.

³¹ "Simon, Simon, Satan has asked to sift all of you as wheat. ³² **But I have prayed for you, Simon, that your faith may not fail. And when you have turned back, strengthen your brothers."**

³³ But he replied, "Lord, I am ready to go with you to prison and to death."

³⁴ Jesus answered, "I tell you, Peter, before the rooster crows today, you will deny three times that you know me."

He prayed for Himself just prior to His death as recorded in Luke Chapter 22.

³⁹ Jesus went out as usual to the Mount of Olives, and his disciples followed him. ⁴⁰ On reaching the place, he said to them, "Pray that you will not fall into temptation." ⁴¹ **He withdrew about a stone's throw beyond them, knelt down and prayed, ⁴² "Father, if you are willing, take this cup from me; yet not my will, but yours be done."** ⁴³ An angel from heaven appeared to him and strengthened him. ⁴⁴ **And being in anguish, he prayed more earnestly, and his sweat was like drops of blood falling to the ground.**

⁴⁵ When he rose from prayer and went back to the disciples, he found them asleep, exhausted from sorrow. ⁴⁶ "Why are you sleeping?" he asked them. "Get up and pray so that you will not fall into temptation."

He prayed for the mission God had given Him in John Chapter 17.

After Jesus said this, he looked toward heaven and prayed:

"Father, the hour has come. Glorify your Son, that your Son may glorify you. ² For you granted him authority over all people that he might give eternal life to all those you have given him. ³ Now this is eternal life: that they know you, the only true God, and Jesus Christ, whom you have sent. ⁴ I have brought you glory on earth by finishing the work you gave me to do. ⁵ And now, Father, glorify me in your presence with the glory I had with you before the world began. ⁶ **"I have revealed you to those whom you gave me out of the world. They were yours; you gave them to me and they have obeyed your word. ⁷ Now they know that**

everything you have given me comes from you. ⁸**For I gave them the words you gave me and they accepted them.** They knew with certainty that I came from you, and they believed that you sent me.

⁹ I pray for them. I am not praying for the world, but for those you have given me, for they are yours. ¹⁰ All I have is yours, and all you have is mine. And glory has come to me through them. ¹¹ I will remain in the world no longer, but they are still in the world, and I am coming to you. Holy Father, protect them by the power of your name, the name you gave me, so that they may be one as we are one.

¹² While I was with them, I protected them and kept them safe by that name you gave me. None has been lost except the one doomed to destruction so that Scripture would be fulfilled. ¹³ "I am coming to you now, but I say these things while I am still in the world, so that they may have the full measure of my joy within them. ¹⁴ I have given them your word and the world has hated them, for they are not of the world any more than I am of the world.

¹⁵ **My prayer is not that you take them out of the world but that you protect them from the evil one.** ¹⁶ **They are not of the world, even as I am not of it.** ¹⁷ **Sanctify them by the truth; your word is truth.** ¹⁸ As you sent me into the world, I have sent them into the world. ¹⁹ For them I sanctify myself, that they too may be truly sanctified.

²⁰ **"My prayer is not for them alone. I pray also for those who will believe in me through their message,** ²¹ **that all of them may be one, Father, just as you are in me and I am in you. May they also be in us so that the world may believe that you have sent me.**

²² I have given them the glory that you gave me, that they may be one as we are one — ²³ I in them and you in me — so that they may be brought to complete unity. Then the world will know that you sent me and have loved them even as you have loved me.

²⁴ **"Father, I want those you have given me to be with me where I am, and to see my glory, the glory you have given me because you loved me before the creation of the world**. ²⁵ "Righteous Father, though the world does not know you, I know you, and they know that you have sent me. ²⁶ I have made you known to them, and will continue to make you known in order that the love you have for me may be in them and that I myself may be in them."

He Built a Team

In Mark Chapter 1, we find an account of Jesus selecting His team and providing them His vision.

¹⁶ As Jesus walked beside the Sea of Galilee, he saw Simon and his brother Andrew casting a net into the lake, for they were fishermen. ¹⁷ **"Come, follow me," Jesus said, "and I will send you out to fish for people."** ¹⁸ At once they left their nets and followed him.

¹⁹ When he had gone a little farther, he saw James son of Zebedee and his brother John in a boat, preparing their nets. ²⁰ Without delay he called them, and they left their father Zebedee in the boat with the hired men and followed him.

In Matthew Chapter 10, we find an account of Jesus sending His men out on a mission of evangelism while He is still with them. In some ways this is a training mission so He can help them get prepared for even a greater task when He is no longer with them.

Notice how Jesus

1. empowers them

2. clarifies the task

3. cautions them about obstacles and

4. assures them that the Spirit will be with them in their time of need.

Jesus called his twelve disciples to him and gave them authority to drive out impure spirits and to heal every disease and sickness.

² These are the names of the twelve apostles: first, Simon (who is called Peter) and his brother Andrew; James son of Zebedee, and his brother John; ³ Philip and Bartholomew; Thomas and Matthew the tax collector; James son of Alphaeus, and Thaddaeus; ⁴ Simon the Zealot and Judas Iscariot, who betrayed him.

⁵ **These twelve Jesus sent out with the following instructions: "Do not go among the Gentiles or enter any town of the Samaritans. ⁶ Go rather to the lost sheep of Israel. ⁷ As you go, proclaim this message: 'The kingdom of heaven has come near.' ⁸ Heal the sick, raise the dead, cleanse those who have leprosy, drive out demons. Freely you have received; freely give.**

⁹ "Do not get any gold or silver or copper to take with you in your belts — ¹⁰ no bag for the journey or extra shirt or sandals or a staff, for the worker is worth his keep.
¹¹ Whatever town or village you enter, search there for some worthy person and stay at their house until you leave. ¹² As you enter the home, give it your greeting. ¹³ **If the home is deserving, let your peace rest on it; if it is not, let your peace return to you. ¹⁴ If anyone will not welcome you or**

listen to your words, leave that home or town and shake the dust off your feet. ¹⁵ Truly I tell you, it will be more bearable for Sodom and Gomorrah on the day of judgment than for that town.

¹⁶ **"I am sending you out like sheep among wolves. Therefore be as shrewd as snakes and as innocent as doves.** ¹⁷ **Be on your guard; you will be handed over to the local councils and be flogged in the synagogues.** ¹⁸ **On my account you will be brought before governors and kings as witnesses to them and to the Gentiles.** ¹⁹ **But when they arrest you, do not worry about what to say or how to say it. At that time you will be given what to say,** ²⁰ **for it will not be you speaking, but the Spirit of your Father speaking through you.**

²¹ "Brother will betray brother to death, and a father his child; children will rebel against their parents and have them put to death. ²² You will be hated by everyone because of me, but the one who stands firm to the end will be saved. ²³ When you are persecuted in one place, flee to another. Truly I tell you, you will not finish going through the towns of Israel before the Son of Man comes.

²⁴ "The student is not above the teacher, nor a servant above his master. ²⁵ It is enough for students to be like their teachers, and servants like their masters. If the head of the house has been called Beelzebul, how much more the members of his household!

²⁶ "So do not be afraid of them, for there is nothing concealed that will not be disclosed, or hidden that will not be made known. ²⁷ What I tell you in the dark, speak in the daylight; what is whispered in your ear, proclaim from the roofs. ²⁸ Do not be afraid of those who kill the body but cannot kill the soul. Rather, be afraid of the One who can destroy both soul and body in hell. ²⁹ Are not two sparrows sold for a penny? Yet not one of them will fall to the ground

outside your Father's care. [30] And even the very hairs of your head are all numbered. [31] So don't be afraid; you are worth more than many sparrows. [32] "Whoever acknowledges me before others, I will also acknowledge before my Father in heaven. [33] But whoever disowns me before others, I will disown before my Father in heaven.

In John Chapter 13, we find an account of Jesus doing the unthinkable as an example to His team. He completely humbled himself to set an example for them. This was the beginning of servant leadership as we know it today.

It was just before the Passover Festival. Jesus knew that the hour had come for him to leave this world and go to the Father. Having loved his own who were in the world, he loved them to the end.

[2] The evening meal was in progress, and the devil had already prompted Judas, the son of Simon Iscariot, to betray Jesus. [3] Jesus knew that the Father had put all things under his power, and that he had come from God and was returning to God; [4] so he got up from the meal, took off his outer clothing, and wrapped a towel around his waist. [5] **After that, he poured water into a basin and began to wash his disciples' feet, drying them with the towel that was wrapped around him.**

[6] He came to Simon Peter, who said to him, "Lord, are you going to wash my feet?"

[7] Jesus replied, "You do not realize now what I am doing, but later you will understand."

[8] **"No," said Peter, "you shall never wash my feet."**

Jesus answered, "Unless I wash you, you have no part with me."

⁹ "Then, Lord," Simon Peter replied, "not just my feet but my hands and my head as well!"

¹⁰ Jesus answered, "Those who have had a bath need only to wash their feet; their whole body is clean. And you are clean, though not every one of you." ¹¹ For he knew who was going to betray him, and that was why he said not every one was clean.

¹² When he had finished washing their feet, he put on his clothes and returned to his place. "Do you understand what I have done for you?" he asked them. ¹³ "You call me 'Teacher' and 'Lord,' and rightly so, for that is what I am. ¹⁴ Now that I, your Lord and Teacher, have washed your feet, you also should wash one another's feet. ¹⁵ I have set you an example that you should do as I have done for you. ¹⁶ Very truly I tell you, no servant is greater than his master, nor is a messenger greater than the one who sent him. ¹⁷ Now that you know these things, you will be blessed if you do them.

The record of the activities at this Passover meal continues in Matthew Chapter 26 as follows. Here Jesus introduces a sacrament (a tradition) which is meant to provide His team with a way of remembering what He has done and will do for them.

¹⁷On the first day of the Festival of Unleavened Bread, the disciples came to Jesus and asked, "Where do you want us to make preparations for you to eat the Passover?"

¹⁸ He replied, "Go into the city to a certain man and tell him, 'The Teacher says: My appointed time is near. I am going to celebrate the Passover with my disciples at your house.'" ¹⁹ So the disciples did as Jesus had directed them and prepared the Passover.

20 When evening came, Jesus was reclining at the table with the Twelve. 21 And while they were eating, he said, "Truly I tell you, one of you will betray me."

22 They were very sad and began to say to him one after the other, "Surely you don't mean me, Lord?"

23 Jesus replied, "The one who has dipped his hand into the bowl with me will betray me. 24 The Son of Man will go just as it is written about him. But woe to that man who betrays the Son of Man! It would be better for him if he had not been born."

25 Then Judas, the one who would betray him, said, "Surely you don't mean me, Rabbi?"

Jesus answered, "You have said so."

26 **While they were eating, Jesus took bread, and when he had given thanks, he broke it and gave it to his disciples, saying, "Take and eat; this is my body."**

27 **Then he took a cup, and when he had given thanks, he gave it to them, saying, "Drink from it, all of you. 28 This is my blood of the covenant, which is poured out for many for the forgiveness of sins. 29 I tell you, I will not drink from this fruit of the vine from now on until that day when I drink it new with you in my Father's kingdom."**

30 When they had sung a hymn, they went out to the Mount of Olives.

In Matthew Chapter 28, Jesus gives His team His final and greatest charge in the following well-known passage. Notice His charge to them and His promise to them.

16 Then the eleven disciples went to Galilee, to the mountain where Jesus had told them to go. 17 When they saw him, they worshiped him; but some doubted. 18 **Then Jesus came**

to them and said, "All authority in heaven and on earth has been given to me. ¹⁹ Therefore go and make disciples of all nations, baptizing them in the name of the Father and of the Son and of the Holy Spirit, ²⁰ and teaching them to obey everything I have commanded you. And surely I am with you always, to the very end of the age."

He Taught

In addition to teaching His team, He also taught the public in general. He began His teaching career at a very early age as recorded in Luke Chapter 2. In this passage, notice His message and the change in the people's response to His teaching!

⁴¹Every year Jesus' parents went to Jerusalem for the Festival of the Passover. ⁴² When he was twelve years old, they went up to the festival, according to the custom. ⁴³ After the festival was over, while his parents were returning home, the boy Jesus stayed behind in Jerusalem, but they were unaware of it. ⁴⁴ Thinking he was in their company, they traveled on for a day. Then they began looking for him among their relatives and friends.

⁴⁵ When they did not find him, they went back to Jerusalem to look for him. ⁴⁶ After three days they found him in the temple courts, sitting among the teachers, listening to them and asking them questions. ⁴⁷ Everyone who heard him was amazed at his understanding and his answers. ⁴⁸ When his parents saw him, they were astonished. His mother said to him, "Son, why have you treated us like this? Your father and I have been anxiously searching for you."

⁴⁹ "Why were you searching for me?" he asked. "Didn't you know I had to be in my Father's house?" ⁵⁰ But they did not understand what he was saying to them.

Jesus returned from the wilderness and began His teaching ministry as recorded in Luke 4.

[14]Jesus returned to Galilee in the power of the Spirit, and news about him spread through the whole countryside. **[15] He was teaching in their synagogues, and everyone praised him.**

[16] He went to Nazareth, where he had been brought up, and on the Sabbath day he went into the synagogue, as was his custom. He stood up to read, [17] and the scroll of the prophet Isaiah was handed to him. Unrolling it, he found the place where it is written:

[18] "The Spirit of the Lord is on me,
because he has anointed me
to proclaim good news to the poor.
He has sent me to proclaim freedom for the prisoners
and recovery of sight for the blind,
to set the oppressed free,
[19]   to proclaim the year of the Lord's favor."

[20] Then he rolled up the scroll, gave it back to the attendant and sat down. The eyes of everyone in the synagogue were fastened on him. [21] He began by saying to them, "Today this scripture is fulfilled in your hearing."

[22] All spoke well of him and were amazed at the gracious words that came from his lips. "Isn't this Joseph's son?" they asked.

[23] Jesus said to them, "Surely you will quote this proverb to me: 'Physician, heal yourself!' And you will tell me, 'Do here in your hometown what we have heard that you did in Capernaum.'"

[24] "Truly I tell you," he continued, "no prophet is accepted in his hometown. [25] I assure you that there were many

widows in Israel in Elijah's time, when the sky was shut for three and a half years and there was a severe famine throughout the land. ²⁶ Yet Elijah was not sent to any of them, but to a widow in Zarephath in the region of Sidon. ²⁷ And there were many in Israel with leprosy in the time of Elisha the prophet, yet not one of them was cleansed — only Naaman the Syrian."

²⁸ All the people in the synagogue were furious when they heard this. ²⁹ They got up, drove him out of the town, and took him to the brow of the hill on which the town was built, in order to throw him off the cliff. ³⁰ But he walked right through the crowd and went on his way.

It would be difficult and presumptive to single out one of Jesus' teachings as the most important...they are all from God. However, I will point to one as a significant example of His teaching: the Sermon on the Mount. I will use the account of this teaching recorded in Matthew Chapters 5 through 7 as follows. I have included only the beginning and end of this passage here.

Chapter 5 (beginning)

Now when Jesus saw the crowds, he went up on a mountainside and sat down. His disciples came to him, ² and he began to teach them.

He said:

³ "Blessed are the poor in spirit,
　　for theirs is the kingdom of heaven.
⁴ Blessed are those who mourn,
　　for they will be comforted.
⁵ Blessed are the meek,
　　for they will inherit the earth.

⁶ Blessed are those who hunger and thirst for righteousness,
   for they will be filled.
⁷ Blessed are the merciful,
   for they will be shown mercy.
⁸ Blessed are the pure in heart,
   for they will see God.
⁹ Blessed are the peacemakers,
   for they will be called children of God.
¹⁰ Blessed are those who are persecuted because of righteousness,
   for theirs is the kingdom of heaven.

¹¹ "Blessed are you when people insult you, persecute you and falsely say all kinds of evil against you because of me. ¹² Rejoice and be glad, because great is your reward in heaven, for in the same way they persecuted the prophets who were before you.

Chapter 7 *(conclusion)*

²⁸ When Jesus had finished saying these things, the crowds were amazed at his teaching, ²⁹ because he taught as one who had authority, and not as their teachers of the law.

He taught them (and us) in many parables. Matthew records another example in Chapter 13 of how Jesus taught using a parable.

That same day Jesus went out of the house and sat by the lake. **² Such large crowds gathered around him that he got into a boat and sat in it, while all the people stood on the shore. ³ Then he told them many things in parables, saying:** "A farmer went out to sow his seed. ⁴ As he was scattering the seed, some fell along the path, and the birds came and ate it up. ⁵ Some fell on rocky places, where it did not have much soil. It sprang up quickly, because the soil was shallow. ⁶ But when the sun came up, the plants were scorched, and they withered because they had no root. ⁷ Other seed fell among thorns, which grew up and choked the plants. ⁸ Still other seed fell on good soil, where it produced a crop—a hundred, sixty or thirty times what was sown. ⁹ Whoever has ears, let them hear."

¹⁰ The disciples came to him and asked, "Why do you speak to the people in parables?"

¹¹ He replied, "Because the knowledge of the secrets of the kingdom of heaven has been given to you, but not to them. ¹² Whoever has will be given more, and they will have an abundance. Whoever does not have, even what they have will be taken from them. ¹³ This is why I speak to them in parables:

"Though seeing, they do not see;
though hearing, they do not hear or understand.

¹⁴ In them is fulfilled the prophecy of Isaiah:

"'You will be ever hearing but never understanding;
you will be ever seeing but never perceiving.
¹⁵ For this people's heart has become calloused;
they hardly hear with their ears,
and they have closed their eyes.
Otherwise they might see with their eyes,
hear with their ears,
understand with their hearts
and turn, and I would heal them.' ¹⁶ But blessed are your eyes because they see, and your ears because they hear. ¹⁷ For truly I tell you, many prophets and righteous people longed to see what you see but did not see it, and to hear what you hear but did not hear it.

Scholars have written extensively on the subject of Jesus' parables. While I certainly have not examined all the writings on this topic, I highly recommend *The Parables of Jesus* by James Montgomery Boice.

Jesus' last public teaching is recorded in John Chapter 12 as follows.

> [44] Then Jesus cried out, "Whoever believes in me does not believe in me only, but in the one who sent me. [45] The one who looks at me is seeing the one who sent me. [46] I have come into the world as a light, so that no one who believes in me should stay in darkness.

> [47] "If anyone hears my words but does not keep them, I do not judge that person. For I did not come to judge the world, but to save the world. [48] There is a judge for the one who rejects me and does not accept my words; the very words I have spoken will condemn them at the last day. **[49] For I did not speak on my own, but the Father who sent me commanded me to say all that I have spoken. [50] I know that his command leads to eternal life. So whatever I say is just what the Father has told me to say."**

He Performed Miracles (signs)

Miracles performed by Jesus are recorded in all the gospels. However, I have confined the following examples to the gospel of John because of what John says in his gospel (John 20:30 – 31).

> "Jesus performed many other signs in the presence of his disciples, which are not recorded in this book. **But these are written that you may believe that Jesus is the Messiah, the Son of God, and that by believing you may have life in his name."**

Following are eight miracles recorded in the gospel of John.

Turning Water into Wine (John 2: 1 – 11)

On the third day a wedding took place at Cana in Galilee. Jesus' mother was there, 2 and Jesus and his disciples had also been invited to the wedding. 3 When the wine was gone, Jesus' mother said to him, "They have no more wine."

4 "Woman, why do you involve me?" Jesus replied. "My hour has not yet come."

5 His mother said to the servants, "Do whatever he tells you."

6 Nearby stood six stone water jars, the kind used by the Jews for ceremonial washing, each holding from twenty to thirty gallons.

7 **Jesus said to the servants, "Fill the jars with water"; so they filled them to the brim.**

8 Then he told them, "Now draw some out and take it to the master of the banquet."

They did so, 9 and the master of the banquet tasted the water that had been turned into wine. He did not realize where it had come from, though the servants who had drawn the water knew. Then he called the bridegroom aside 10 and said, "Everyone brings out the choice wine first and then the cheaper wine after the guests have had too much to drink; but you have saved the best till now."

11 **What Jesus did here in Cana of Galilee was the first of the signs through which he revealed his glory; and his disciples believed in him.**

Healing the Official's Son (John 4: 46 – 54)

46 Once more he visited Cana in Galilee, where he had turned the water into wine. And there was a certain royal official whose son lay sick at Capernaum. 47 When this man heard that Jesus had arrived in Galilee from Judea, he went to him and begged him to come and heal his son, who was close to death.

48 "Unless you people see signs and wonders," Jesus told him, "you will never believe."

49 The royal official said, "Sir, come down before my child dies."

50 "Go," Jesus replied, "your son will live."

The man took Jesus at his word and departed. 51 While he was still on the way, his servants met him with the news that his boy was living. 52 When he inquired as to the time when his son got better, they said to him, "Yesterday, at one in the afternoon, the fever left him."

53 Then the father realized that this was the exact time at which Jesus had said to him, "Your son will live." So he and his whole household believed.

54 This was the second sign Jesus performed after coming from Judea to Galilee.

Healing the Paralytic (John 5: 1 – 9)

Some time later, Jesus went up to Jerusalem for one of the Jewish festivals. 2 Now there is in Jerusalem near the Sheep Gate a pool, which in Aramaic is called Bethesda and which is surrounded by five covered colonnades. 3 Here a great number of disabled people used to lie — the blind, the lame, the paralyzed. 5 One who was there had been an invalid for thirty-eight years. 6 When Jesus saw him lying there and learned that he had been in this condition for a long time, he asked him, "Do you want to get well?"

⁷ "Sir," the invalid replied, "I have no one to help me into the pool when the water is stirred. While I am trying to get in, someone else goes down ahead of me."

⁸ **Then Jesus said to him, "Get up! Pick up your mat and walk."** ⁹ **At once the man was cured; he picked up his mat and walked.**

Feeding 5,000 (John 6: 1 – 14)

Some time after this, Jesus crossed to the far shore of the Sea of Galilee (that is, the Sea of Tiberias), ² and a great crowd of people followed him because they saw the signs he had performed by healing the sick. ³ Then Jesus went up on a mountainside and sat down with his disciples. ⁴ The Jewish Passover Festival was near.

⁵ When Jesus looked up and saw a great crowd coming toward him, he said to Philip, "Where shall we buy bread for these people to eat?" ⁶ He asked this only to test him, for he already had in mind what he was going to do.

⁷ Philip answered him, "It would take more than half a year's wages to buy enough bread for each one to have a bite!"

⁸ Another of his disciples, Andrew, Simon Peter's brother, spoke up, ⁹ "Here is a boy with five small barley loaves and two small fish, but how far will they go among so many?"

¹⁰ Jesus said, "Have the people sit down." There was plenty of grass in that place, and they sat down (about five thousand men were there). ¹¹ Jesus then took the loaves, gave thanks, and distributed to those who were seated as much as they wanted. He did the same with the fish.

¹² **When they had all had enough to eat, he said to his disciples, "Gather the pieces that are left over. Let**

nothing be wasted." ¹³ So they gathered them and filled twelve baskets with the pieces of the five barley loaves left over by those who had eaten.

¹⁴ After the people saw the sign Jesus performed, they began to say, "Surely this is the Prophet who is to come into the world." ¹⁵ Jesus, knowing that they intended to come and make him king by force, withdrew again to a mountain by himself.

Walking on Water (John 6: 16 – 21)

When evening came, his disciples went down to the lake, ¹⁷ where they got into a boat and set off across the lake for Capernaum. By now it was dark, and Jesus had not yet joined them. ¹⁸ A strong wind was blowing and the waters grew rough. ¹⁹ When they had rowed about three or four miles, **they saw Jesus approaching the boat, walking on the water; and they were frightened.** ²⁰ But he said to them, "It is I; don't be afraid." ²¹ Then they were willing to take him into the boat, and immediately the boat reached the shore where they were heading.

Healing the Blind Man (John 9: 1 – 12)

As he went along, he saw a man blind from birth. ² His disciples asked him, "Rabbi, who sinned, this man or his parents, that he was born blind?"

³ "Neither this man nor his parents sinned," said Jesus, "but this happened so that the works of God might be displayed in him. ⁴ As long as it is day, we must do the works of him who sent me. Night is coming, when no one can work. ⁵ While I am in the world, I am the light of the world."

⁶ **After saying this, he spit on the ground, made some mud with the saliva, and put it on the man's eyes.** ⁷ **"Go," he told him, "wash in the Pool of Siloam" (this word means "Sent"). So the man went and washed, and came home seeing.**

⁸ His neighbors and those who had formerly seen him begging asked, "Isn't this the same man who used to sit and beg?" ⁹ Some claimed that he was.

Others said, "No, he only looks like him."

But he himself insisted, "I am the man."

¹⁰ "How then were your eyes opened?" they asked.

¹¹ He replied, "The man they call Jesus made some mud and put it on my eyes. He told me to go to Siloam and wash. So I went and washed, and then I could see."

¹² "Where is this man?" they asked him.

"I don't know," he said.

Raising Lazarus from the Dead (John 11: 38 – 44)

³⁸ Jesus, once more deeply moved, came to the tomb. It was a cave with a stone laid across the entrance. ³⁹ "Take away the stone," he said.

"But Lord," said Martha, the sister of the dead man, "by this time there is a bad odor, for he has been there four days."

⁴⁰ Then Jesus said, "Did I not tell you that if you believe, you will see the glory of God?"

⁴¹ So they took away the stone. Then Jesus looked up and said, "Father, I thank you that you have heard me. ⁴² I knew that you always hear me, but I said this for the benefit of the people standing here, that they may believe that you sent me."

⁴³ When he had said this, Jesus called in a loud voice, "Lazarus, come out!" ⁴⁴ The dead man came out, his hands and feet wrapped with strips of linen, and a cloth around his face.

Jesus said to them, "Take off the grave clothes and let him go."

Catching Fish (John 21: 1 – 6)

Afterward Jesus appeared again to his disciples, by the Sea of Galilee. It happened this way: ² Simon Peter, Thomas (also known as Didymus), Nathanael from Cana in Galilee, the sons of Zebedee, and two other disciples were together. ³ "I'm going out to fish," Simon Peter told them, and they said, "We'll go with you." So they went out and got into the boat, but that night they caught nothing.

⁴ Early in the morning, Jesus stood on the shore, but the disciples did not realize that it was Jesus.

⁵ He called out to them, "Friends, haven't you any fish?"

"No," they answered.

⁶ He said, "Throw your net on the right side of the boat and you will find some." When they did, they were unable to haul the net in because of the large number of fish.

Significance of the Signs (Miracles)

On several occasions, John records this similar pattern … They saw the sign (miracle) and then believed. This process of conversion through seeing and then believing can be found in

John 2: 11

John 4: 39 – 42

John 4: 51 - 53

John 6: 14 – 15

In John Chapter 10, Jesus gets into a confrontation with the Jewish leaders at the Festival of Dedication because of His claims about Himself. And, He says the following about His works.

> 22 Then came the Festival of Dedication at Jerusalem. It was winter, 23 and Jesus was in the temple courts walking in Solomon's Colonnade. 24 The Jews who were there gathered around him, saying, "How long will you keep us in suspense? If you are the Messiah, tell us plainly."
>
> 25 Jesus answered, "I did tell you, but you do not believe. **The works I do in my Father's name testify about me, 26 but you do not believe because you are not my sheep. 27 My sheep listen to my voice; I know them, and they follow me. 28 I give them eternal life, and they shall never perish; no one will snatch them out of my hand. 29 My Father, who has given them to me, is greater than all; no one can snatch them out of my Father's hand. 30 I and the Father are one."**
>
> 31 Again his Jewish opponents picked up stones to stone him, 32 but Jesus said to them, "I have shown you many good works from the Father. For which of these do you stone me?"
>
> 33 "We are not stoning you for any good work," they replied, "but for blasphemy, because you, a mere man, claim to be God."

Even though they are ready to stone Him, Jesus continues to encourage them to believe by pointing to the significance of the works (signs).

³⁴ Jesus answered them, "Is it not written in your Law, 'I have said you are "gods"'? ³⁵ If he called them 'gods,' to whom the word of God came — and Scripture cannot be set aside — ³⁶ what about the one whom the Father set apart as his very own and sent into the world? Why then do you accuse me of blasphemy because I said, 'I am God's Son'? ³⁷ Do not believe me unless I do the works of my Father. **³⁸ But if I do them, even though you do not believe me, believe the works, that you may know and understand that the Father is in me, and I in the Father." ³⁹ Again they tried to seize him, but he escaped their grasp.**

John concludes this chapter with a surprising account of many believing in Him.

⁴⁰ Then Jesus went back across the Jordan to the place where John had been baptizing in the early days. There he stayed, ⁴¹ and many people came to him. They said, **"Though John never performed a sign, all that John said about this man was true." ⁴² And in that place many believed in Jesus.**

John Piper has a wonderful teaching on this passage. He indicates the reason John the Baptist did no signs was that he, John the Baptist, was a sign for the people since he humbled himself relative to Jesus.

An example for our times

When I was writing this work, the United States had just completed the 58th presidential election. This election was quite unusual and difficult in terms of the promises made and the negative rhetoric. As Ms. Clinton and Mr. Trump campaigned throughout the country, they did everything they could to increase their followings. They both made a number of significant promises which they thought voters wanted to hear. I (and most likely many others) wondered if they could or would fulfill these promises. But the point is that they said whatever they thought was necessary to encourage people to follow them.

Such was not the case with Jesus.

While Jesus did perform miracles that inspired conversions, He was brutally honest about people following Him and did not just tell people what they wanted to hear. Consider this example from Luke 14.

> 25 Large crowds were traveling with Jesus, and turning to them he said: 26 "If anyone comes to me and does not hate father and mother, wife and children, brothers and sisters—yes, even their own life—such a person cannot be my disciple. 27 And whoever does not carry their cross and follow me cannot be my disciple.
>
> 28 "Suppose one of you wants to build a tower. Won't you first sit down and estimate the cost to see if you have enough money to complete it? 29 For if you lay the foundation and are not able to finish it, everyone who sees it will ridicule you, 30 saying, 'This person began to build and wasn't able to finish.'
>
> 31 "Or suppose a king is about to go to war against another king. Won't he first sit down and consider whether he is able with ten thousand men to oppose the one coming against him with twenty thousand? 32 If he is not able, he will send a delegation while the other is still a long way off and will ask for terms of peace. 33 In the same way, those of you who do not give up everything you have cannot be my disciples.

³⁴ "Salt is good, but if it loses its saltiness, how can it be made salty again? ³⁵ It is fit neither for the soil nor for the manure pile; it is thrown out.

"Whoever has ears to hear, let them hear."

In this account, Jesus already has large crowds following Him. Luke does not say whether it is due to signs or teachings...I suspect both. But the important point is Jesus' reaction to seeing the large crowds of followers. He wants them to understand the real costs of following Him. He does not want them to be lured into following based on signs or promises of prosperity. He wants them to understand (count) that following Him will come at a personal cost.

Oh that our politicians and all of us would learn from this example!

The miracles of forgiveness
In addition to these physical miracles, Jesus performed spiritual miracles by forgiving people of their sins. Two examples are the woman caught in adultery (John 8) and the thief on the cross as recorded in Luke 23.

John 8

At dawn he appeared again in the temple courts, where all the people gathered around him, and he sat down to teach them. ³ The teachers of the law and the Pharisees brought in a woman caught in adultery. They made her stand before the group ⁴ and said to Jesus, "Teacher, this woman was caught in the act of adultery. ⁵ In the Law Moses commanded us to stone such women. Now what do you say?" ⁶ They were using this question as a trap, in order to have a basis for accusing him.

But Jesus bent down and started to write on the ground with his finger. 7 When they kept on questioning him, he straightened up and said to them, "Let any one of you who is without sin be the first to throw a stone at her." 8 Again he stooped down and wrote on the ground.

9 At this, those who heard began to go away one at a time, the older ones first, until only Jesus was left, with the woman still standing there. 10 Jesus straightened up and asked her, "Woman, where are they? Has no one condemned you?"

11 "No one, sir," she said.

"Then neither do I condemn you," Jesus declared. "Go now and leave your life of sin."

Luke 23

32 Two other men, both criminals, were also led out with him to be executed. 33 When they came to the place called the Skull, they crucified him there, along with the criminals — one on his right, the other on his left. 34 Jesus said, "Father, forgive them, for they do not know what they are doing." And they divided up his clothes by casting lots.

35 The people stood watching, and the rulers even sneered at him. They said, "He saved others; let him save himself if he is God's Messiah, the Chosen One."

36 The soldiers also came up and mocked him. They offered him wine vinegar 37 and said, "If you are the king of the Jews, save yourself."

38 There was a written notice above him, which read: THIS IS THE KING OF THE JEWS.

39 One of the criminals who hung there hurled insults at him: "Aren't you the Messiah? Save yourself and us!"

⁴⁰ But the other criminal rebuked him. "Don't you fear God," he said, "since you are under the same sentence? ⁴¹ We are punished justly, for we are getting what our deeds deserve. But this man has done nothing wrong."

⁴² Then he said, "Jesus, remember me when you come into your kingdom."

⁴³ Jesus answered him, "Truly I tell you, today you will be with me in paradise."

Obeying His Father

Jesus carried out the plan of His Father by doing exactly what His Father wanted done. We see this in three passages from John as follows.

John 5

¹⁹ Jesus gave them this answer: **"Very truly I tell you, the Son can do nothing by himself; he can do only what he sees his Father doing, because whatever the Father does the Son also does.** ²⁰ For the Father loves the Son and shows him all he does. Yes, and he will show him even greater works than these, so that you will be amazed. ²¹ For just as the Father raises the dead and gives them life, even so the Son gives life to whom he is pleased to give it. ²² Moreover, the Father judges no one, but has entrusted all judgment to the Son, ²³ that all may honor the Son just as they honor the Father. Whoever does not honor the Son does not honor the Father, who sent him.

John 8

²⁷ They did not understand that he was telling them about his Father. ²⁸ So Jesus said, "When you have lifted up the Son of Man, then you will know that I am he and that **I do**

nothing on my own but speak just what the Father has taught me.

29 The one who sent me is with me; he has not left me alone, for I always do what pleases him." 30 Even as he spoke, many believed in him.

John 17

After Jesus said this, he looked toward heaven and prayed,

"Father, the hour has come. Glorify your Son, that your Son may glorify you. 2 For you granted him authority over all people that he might give eternal life to all those you have given him.

3 Now this is eternal life: that they know you, the only true God, and Jesus Christ, whom you have sent. **4 I have brought you glory on earth by finishing the work you gave me to do.** 5 And now, Father, glorify me in your presence with the glory I had with you before the world began.

Luke records an example of Jesus' obedience in Chapter 22.

39 Jesus went out as usual to the Mount of Olives, and his disciples followed him. 40 On reaching the place, he said to them, "Pray that you will not fall into temptation." 41 He withdrew about a stone's throw beyond them, knelt down and prayed, **42 "Father, if you are willing, take this cup from me; yet not my will, but yours be done."** 43 An angel from heaven appeared to him and strengthened him. 44 And being in anguish, he prayed more earnestly, and his sweat was like drops of blood falling to the ground.

45 When he rose from prayer and went back to the disciples, he found them asleep, exhausted from sorrow. 46 "Why are

you sleeping?" he asked them. "Get up and pray so that you will not fall into temptation."

The ultimate act of obedience was His crucifixion. We have the following account of His death in Luke Chapter 23.

> [44] It was now about noon, and darkness came over the whole land until three in the afternoon, [45] for the sun stopped shining. And the curtain of the temple was torn in two. [46] Jesus called out with a loud voice, **"Father, into your hands I commit my spirit." When he had said this, he breathed his last.**
>
> [47] The centurion, seeing what had happened, praised God and said, "Surely this was a righteous man." [48] When all the people who had gathered to witness this sight saw what took place, they beat their breasts and went away. [49] But all those who knew him, including the women who had followed him from Galilee, stood at a distance, watching these things.

But the crucifixion of Jesus was not the end. For Christians, it is the prelude to a new beginning.

So far we have looked at who He is and what He did. In Chapter 3, we will look at one more thing before we examine the significance of His activities for me.

Chapter 3
One More Thing!

In addition to the signs and claims we reviewed in Chapter 2, there is one more thing!

He was raised from the dead! What greater sign could there be that attests to Jesus being the Son of God? Let's examine this climactic event and then look at what all His resurrection means for me in the Chapter 4.

It is both interesting and affirming that all four gospels (Matthew, Mark, Luke, and John) contain accounts of the resurrection as follows:

> Matthew 27: 62 – 66 and Matthew Chapter 28
> Mark Chapter 16
> Luke Chapter 24
> John 20: 1 – 29 and John Chapter 21.

In addition, Paul records the death and resurrection of Jesus in 1 Corinthians Chapter 15.

> Now, brothers and sisters, I want to remind you of the gospel I preached to you, which you received and on which you have taken your stand. ² By this gospel you are saved, if you hold firmly to the word I preached to you. Otherwise, you have believed in vain.
>
> ³ For what I received I passed on to you as of first importance: that Christ died for our sins according to the Scriptures, **⁴ that he was buried, that he was raised on the third day according to the Scriptures, ⁵ and that he appeared to Cephas, and then to the Twelve. ⁶ After that,**

he appeared to more than five hundred of the brothers and sisters at the same time, most of whom are still living, though some have fallen asleep. ⁷ Then he appeared to James, then to all the apostles, ⁸ and last of all he appeared to me also, as to one abnormally born.

⁹ For I am the least of the apostles and do not even deserve to be called an apostle, because I persecuted the church of God. ¹⁰ But by the grace of God I am what I am, and his grace to me was not without effect. No, I worked harder than all of them — yet not I, but the grace of God that was with me. ¹¹ Whether, then, it is I or they, this is what we preach, and this is what you believed.

Since we have been using John as a primary source, let's look at his account of the resurrection from Chapters 20 and 21.

Chapter 20

Early on the first day of the week, while it was still dark, Mary Magdalene went to the tomb and saw that the stone had been removed from the entrance. ² So she came running to Simon Peter and the other disciple, the one Jesus loved, and said, "They have taken the Lord out of the tomb, and we don't know where they have put him!"

³ So Peter and the other disciple started for the tomb. ⁴ Both were running, but the other disciple outran Peter and reached the tomb first. ⁵ He bent over and looked in at the strips of linen lying there but did not go in. ⁶ Then Simon Peter came along behind him and went straight into the tomb. He saw the strips of linen lying there, ⁷ as well as the cloth that had been wrapped around Jesus' head. The cloth was still lying in its place, separate from the linen. ⁸ Finally the other disciple, who had reached the tomb first, also went inside. He saw and believed. ⁹ (They still did not understand from Scripture that Jesus had to rise from the

dead.) ¹⁰ Then the disciples went back to where they were staying.

¹¹ Now Mary stood outside the tomb crying. As she wept, she bent over to look into the tomb ¹² and saw two angels in white, seated where Jesus' body had been, one at the head and the other at the foot.

¹³ They asked her, "Woman, why are you crying?"

"They have taken my Lord away," she said, "and I don't know where they have put him." ¹⁴ At this, she turned around and saw Jesus standing there, but she did not realize that it was Jesus.

¹⁵ He asked her, "Woman, why are you crying? Who is it you are looking for?"

Thinking he was the gardener, she said, "Sir, if you have carried him away, tell me where you have put him, and I will get him."

¹⁶ Jesus said to her, "Mary."

She turned toward him and cried out in Aramaic, "Rabboni!" (which means "Teacher").

¹⁷ Jesus said, "Do not hold on to me, for I have not yet ascended to the Father. Go instead to my brothers and tell them, 'I am ascending to my Father and your Father, to my God and your God.'"

¹⁸ Mary Magdalene went to the disciples with the news: "I have seen the Lord!" And she told them that he had said these things to her.

¹⁹ **On the evening of that first day of the week, when the disciples were together, with the doors locked for fear of the Jewish leaders, Jesus came and stood among them and said, "Peace be with you!" ²⁰ After he said this, he showed them his hands and side. The disciples were overjoyed when they saw the Lord.**

²¹ Again Jesus said, "Peace be with you! As the Father has sent me, I am sending you." ²² And with that he breathed on them and said, "Receive the Holy Spirit. ²³ If you forgive anyone's sins, their sins are forgiven; if you do not forgive them, they are not forgiven."

²⁴ Now Thomas (also known as Didymus), one of the Twelve, was not with the disciples when Jesus came. ²⁵ So the other disciples told him, "We have seen the Lord!"

But he said to them, "Unless I see the nail marks in his hands and put my finger where the nails were, and put my hand into his side, I will not believe."

²⁶ **A week later his disciples were in the house again, and Thomas was with them. Though the doors were locked, Jesus came and stood among them and said, "Peace be with you!"** ²⁷ **Then he said to Thomas, "Put your finger here; see my hands. Reach out your hand and put it into my side. Stop doubting and believe."**

²⁸ **Thomas said to him, "My Lord and my God!"**

²⁹ Then Jesus told him, "Because you have seen me, you have believed; blessed are those who have not seen and yet have believed."

John's account continues in Chapter 21.

Afterward Jesus appeared again to his disciples, by the Sea of Galilee. It happened this way: ² **Simon Peter, Thomas (also known as Didymus), Nathanael from Cana in Galilee, the sons of Zebedee, and two other disciples were together.** ³ **"I'm going out to fish," Simon Peter told them, and they said, "We'll go with you." So they went out and got into the boat, but that night they caught nothing.**

⁴ Early in the morning, Jesus stood on the shore, but the disciples did not realize that it was Jesus.

⁵ He called out to them, "Friends, haven't you any fish?"

"No," they answered.

⁶ He said, "Throw your net on the right side of the boat and you will find some." When they did, they were unable to haul the net in because of the large number of fish.

⁷ Then the disciple whom Jesus loved said to Peter, "It is the Lord!" As soon as Simon Peter heard him say, "It is the Lord," he wrapped his outer garment around him (for he had taken it off) and jumped into the water. ⁸ The other disciples followed in the boat, towing the net full of fish, for they were not far from shore, about a hundred yards. ⁹ When they landed, they saw a fire of burning coals there with fish on it, and some bread.

¹⁰ Jesus said to them, "Bring some of the fish you have just caught." ¹¹ So Simon Peter climbed back into the boat and dragged the net ashore. It was full of large fish, 153, but even with so many the net was not torn. ¹² Jesus said to them, "Come and have breakfast." None of the disciples dared ask him, "Who are you?" They knew it was the Lord. ¹³ Jesus came, took the bread and gave it to them, and did the same with the fish. **¹⁴ This was now the third time Jesus appeared to his disciples after he was raised from the dead.**

These two accounts from John provide clear records of Jesus appearing to a number of His disciples after being crucified. The resurrection of Jesus is a critical component of the Gospel, as we will see in Chapter 4 when we look at the significance of these events and claims.

Chapter 4

What Does this Mean for Me?

Literally hundreds of places in the Bible provide an answer to this question. First, let's continue in John to look for insight into what this means for me. I want to start in John 3 with one of the most familiar passages in the Bible, John 3:16.

Let's look at that chapter.

John 3

Now there was a Pharisee, a man named Nicodemus who was a member of the Jewish ruling council. ² He came to Jesus at night and said, "Rabbi, we know that you are a teacher who has come from God. For no one could perform the signs you are doing if God were not with him."

³ Jesus replied, "Very truly I tell you, no one can see the kingdom of God unless they are born again."

⁴ "How can someone be born when they are old?" Nicodemus asked. "Surely they cannot enter a second time into their mother's womb to be born!"

⁵ Jesus answered, "Very truly I tell you, no one can enter the kingdom of God unless they are born of water and the Spirit. ⁶ Flesh gives birth to flesh, but the Spirit gives birth to spirit. ⁷ You should not be surprised at my saying, 'You must be born again.' ⁸ The wind blows wherever it pleases. You hear its sound, but you cannot tell where it comes from or where it is going. So it is with everyone born of the Spirit."

⁹ "How can this be?" Nicodemus asked.

¹⁰ "You are Israel's teacher," said Jesus, "and do you not understand these things? ¹¹ Very truly I tell you, we speak

of what we know, and we testify to what we have seen, but still you people do not accept our testimony. [12] I have spoken to you of earthly things and you do not believe; how then will you believe if I speak of heavenly things? [13] No one has ever gone into heaven except the one who came from heaven — the Son of Man. [14] Just as Moses lifted up the snake in the wilderness, so the Son of Man must be lifted up, [15] that everyone who believes may have eternal life in him."

[16] **For God so loved the world that he gave his one and only Son, that whoever believes in him shall not perish but have eternal life. [17] For God did not send his Son into the world to condemn the world, but to save the world through him. [18] Whoever believes in him is not condemned, but whoever does not believe stands condemned already because they have not believed in the name of God's one and only Son. [19] This is the verdict: Light has come into the world, but people loved darkness instead of light because their deeds were evil.** [20] Everyone who does evil hates the light, and will not come into the light for fear that their deeds will be exposed. [21] But whoever lives by the truth comes into the light, so that it may be seen plainly that what they have done has been done in the sight of God.

The conclusions for me from this passage are threefold.

1. Whoever believes in Jesus has eternal life.

2. Jesus is the only way to eternal life for me (also see John 14:6).

3. Without belief (faith) in Him I am condemned.

Let's look at John Chapter 8 for Jesus' additional teaching regarding this.

> 34 Jesus replied, **"Very truly I tell you, everyone who sins is a slave to sin. 35 Now a slave has no permanent place in the family, but a son belongs to it forever. 36 So if the Son sets you free, you will be free indeed.** 37 I know that you are Abraham's descendants. Yet you are looking for a way to kill me, because you have no room for my word. 38 I am telling you what I have seen in the Father's presence, and you are doing what you have heard from your father."

For me, the book of Romans has been extremely helpful regarding the significance of Jesus in my life. I recommend the first seven chapters of Romans in which Paul presents a thorough explanation of my failings and my need to be rescued from my sinful way of life.

This theme, which runs throughout the entire Bible, is also addressed in the gospels and is the primary narrative of the New Testament. My understanding of this theme can be explained in three simple statements.

I am a sinful person.

I stand condemned under the just wrath of God because of my sinfulness.

Jesus came to save me from my sinfulness by standing in my place and receiving the just punishment that I deserve due to my sinfulness.

I recommend John Piper's sermon entitled "The Greatest Thing in the World: An Overview of Romans 1 – 7", which he preached on September 2, 2001 (desiringgod.com). Piper offers an outstanding teaching on the topic of sin and redemption through Jesus Christ.

In addition, let's look again at John Chapter 6.

35 Then Jesus declared, "I am the bread of life. Whoever comes to me will never go hungry, and whoever believes in me will never be thirsty. 36 But as I told you, you have seen me and still you do not believe. 37 **All those the Father gives me will come to me, and whoever comes to me I will never drive away. 38 For I have come down from heaven not to do my will but to do the will of him who sent me. 39 And this is the will of him who sent me, that I shall lose none of all those he has given me, but raise them up at the last day. 40 For my Father's will is that everyone who looks to the Son and believes in him shall have eternal life, and I will raise them up at the last day."**

41 At this the Jews there began to grumble about him because he said, "I am the bread that came down from heaven." 42 They said, "Is this not Jesus, the son of Joseph, whose father and mother we know? How can he now say, 'I came down from heaven'?"

43 "Stop grumbling among yourselves," Jesus answered. 44 **"No one can come to me unless the Father who sent me draws them, and I will raise them up at the last day. 45 It is written in the Prophets: 'They will all be taught by God.' Everyone who has heard the Father and learned from him comes to me.**

46 No one has seen the Father except the one who is from God; only he has seen the Father. 47 Very truly I tell you, the one who believes has eternal life. 48 I am the bread of life.

49 Your ancestors ate the manna in the wilderness, yet they died. 50 But here is the bread that comes down from heaven,

which anyone may eat and not die. [51] I am the living bread that came down from heaven. Whoever eats this bread will live forever. This bread is my flesh, which I will give for the life of the world."

Based on this passage, I conclude the following.

God "gives" (ordains) certain people from all people groups to Jesus for salvation and eternal life. Those individuals "hear" from God and are taught by Him through the Holy Spirit. Jesus "raises them up at the last day," meaning that He brings them to Heaven with Him for eternal life. Paul writes about this in Romans Chapter 4: 1-5.

In my opinion, the writings of Paul (Romans 9) and Peter (1 Peter 1) support this position. Also, Jesus says on more than one occasion that He will grant eternal life.

John Piper has preached a number of sermons on this topic that can be found on the desiringgod.com website. Piper's full inventory is worth exploring and I specifically recommend his sermon on this topic entitled, "I Am the Light of the World" dated March 12, 2011 which is based on John 8: 12 – 30.

In Jesus' high priestly prayer in John 17, note the important distinctions in His prayer. Let's look carefully at verses 6-12.

> [6] "I have revealed you to those whom you gave me out of the world. They were yours; you gave them to me and they have obeyed your word. [7] Now they know that everything you have given me comes from you. [8] For I gave them the words you gave me and they accepted them. They knew with certainty that I came from you, and they believed that you sent me. [9] I pray for them. I am not praying for the world, but for those you have given me,

for they are yours. ¹⁰ All I have is yours, and all you have is mine. And glory has come to me through them. ¹¹ I will remain in the world no longer, but they are still in the world, and I am coming to you. Holy Father, protect them by the power of your name, the name you gave me, so that they may be one as we are one. ¹² **While I was with them, I protected them and kept them safe by that name you gave me. None has been lost except the one doomed to destruction so that Scripture would be fulfilled.**

Now, there is a clear distinction between those given to Jesus by the Father and those who are not. A specific example of this is how Jesus prayed for Peter in the Luke Chapter 22. He did not pray for Judas, Herod, or Pilate. The following passage contains His prayer for Peter.

³¹ "Simon, Simon, Satan has asked to sift all of you as wheat. ³² **But I have prayed for you, Simon, that your faith may not fail. And when you have turned back, strengthen your brothers."**

³³ But he replied, "Lord, I am ready to go with you to prison and to death."

³⁴ Jesus answered, "I tell you, Peter, before the rooster crows today, you will deny three times that you know me."

There are three important aspects of this passage.

First, Jesus knew that Peter would betray Him.
Second, Jesus prayed that he (Peter) would not be lost.
Finally, Jesus knew that Peter would turn back (not be lost).

Jesus' approach to Peter is completely different from His approach to Judas...even though they both denied Him! So my conclusion is that Jesus' approach (given to Him from the Father) is not universally the same for all people.

Also, it is instructive to examine the difference in how Jesus treated the two thieves who were crucified with Him. Let's look at Luke Chapter 23.

> [39] One of the criminals who hung there hurled insults at him: "Aren't you the Messiah? Save yourself and us!"
>
> [40] But the other criminal rebuked him. "Don't you fear God," he said, "since you are under the same sentence? [41] We are punished justly, for we are getting what our deeds deserve. But this man has done nothing wrong."
>
> [42] Then he said, "Jesus, remember me when you come into your kingdom."
>
> [43] Jesus answered him, "Truly I tell you, today you will be with me in paradise."

In Chapter 2 we looked at Jesus' claim that He and the father are one. One of the passages we used to illustrate that claim was from John 10.

> [25] Jesus answered, "I did tell you, but you do not believe. The works I do in my Father's name testify about me, [26] but you do not believe because you are not my sheep. [27] My sheep listen to my voice; I know them, and they follow me. [28] I give them eternal life, and they shall never perish; no one will snatch them out of my hand. [29] My Father, who has given them to me, is greater than all; no one can snatch them out of my Father's hand. [30] I and the Father are one."

What differences does this make for me? I draw a very important conclusion from this passage. If I am "one of His sheep" then I am eternally secure in the Father's hand. Since Jesus and the Father are one, no one can snatch me from Their hand. This is huge!

In Chapter 3, we looked at the resurrection as a significant event in the life of Jesus. What does that event mean for me? Paul's writing in 1 Corinthians Chapter 15 offers guidance.

Now, brothers and sisters, I want to remind you of the gospel I preached to you, which you received and on which you have taken your stand. [2] By this gospel you are saved, if you hold firmly to the word I preached to you. Otherwise, you have believed in vain.

[3] For what I received I passed on to you as of first importance: that Christ died for our sins according to the Scriptures, **[4] that he was buried, that he was raised on the third day according to the Scriptures, [5] and that he appeared to Cephas, and then to the Twelve. [6] After that, he appeared to more than five hundred of the brothers and sisters at the same time, most of whom are still living, though some have fallen asleep. [7] Then he appeared to James, then to all the apostles, [8] and last of all he appeared to me also, as to one abnormally born.**

[9] For I am the least of the apostles and do not even deserve to be called an apostle, because I persecuted the church of God. [10] But by the grace of God I am what I am, and his grace to me was not without effect. No, I worked harder than all of them—yet not I, but the grace of God that was with me. [11] Whether, then, it is I or they, this is what we preach, and this is what you believed.

[12] But if it is preached that Christ has been raised from the dead, **how can some of you say that there is no resurrection of the dead? [13] If there is no resurrection of the dead, then not even Christ has been raised. [14] And if Christ has not been raised, our preaching is useless and so is your faith. [15] More than that, we are then found to be false witnesses about God, for we have testified about God that he raised Christ from the dead. But he did not**

raise him if in fact the dead are not raised. ¹⁶ For if the dead are not raised, then Christ has not been raised either. ¹⁷ And if Christ has not been raised, your faith is futile; you are still in your sins. ¹⁸ Then those also who have fallen asleep in Christ are lost. ¹⁹ If only for this life we have hope in Christ, we are of all people most to be pitied.

²⁰ But Christ has indeed been raised from the dead, the firstfruits of those who have fallen asleep. ²¹ For since death came through a man, the resurrection of the dead comes also through a man. ²² For as in Adam all die, so in Christ all will be made alive. ²³ But each in turn: Christ, the firstfruits; then, when he comes, those who belong to him. ²⁴ Then the end will come, when he hands over the kingdom to God the Father after he has destroyed all dominion, authority and power. ²⁵ For he must reign until he has put all his enemies under his feet. ²⁶ The last enemy to be destroyed is death. ²⁷ For he "has put everything under his feet." Now when it says that "everything" has been put under him, it is clear that this does not include God himself, who put everything under Christ. ²⁸ When he has done this, then the Son himself will be made subject to him who put everything under him, so that God may be all in all.

²⁹ Now if there is no resurrection, what will those do who are baptized for the dead? If the dead are not raised at all, why are people baptized for them? ³⁰ And as for us, why do we endanger ourselves every hour? ³¹ I face death every day — yes, just as surely as I boast about you in Christ Jesus our Lord. ³² If I fought wild beasts in Ephesus with no more than human hopes, what have I gained? If the dead are not raised,

"Let us eat and drink,
for tomorrow we die."

³³ Do not be misled: "Bad company corrupts good character." ³⁴ Come back to your senses as you ought, and stop sinning; for there are some who are ignorant of God — I say this to your shame.

³⁵ But someone will ask, "How are the dead raised? With what kind of body will they come?" ³⁶ How foolish! What you sow does not come to life unless it dies. ³⁷ When you sow, you do not plant the body that will be, but just a seed, perhaps of wheat or of something else. ³⁸ But God gives it a body as he has determined, and to each kind of seed he gives its own body. ³⁹ Not all flesh is the same: People have one kind of flesh, animals have another, birds another and fish another. ⁴⁰ There are also heavenly bodies and there are earthly bodies; but the splendor of the heavenly bodies is one kind, and the splendor of the earthly bodies is another. ⁴¹ The sun has one kind of splendor, the moon another and the stars another; and star differs from star in splendor.

⁴² So will it be with the resurrection of the dead. The body that is sown is perishable, it is raised imperishable; ⁴³ it is sown in dishonor, it is raised in glory; it is sown in weakness, it is raised in power; ⁴⁴ it is sown a natural body, it is raised a spiritual body.

If there is a natural body, there is also a spiritual body. ⁴⁵ So it is written: "The first man Adam became a living being"; the last Adam, a life-giving spirit. ⁴⁶ The spiritual did not come first, but the natural, and after that the spiritual. ⁴⁷ The first man was of the dust of the earth; the second man is of heaven. ⁴⁸ As was the earthly man, so are those who are of the earth; and as is the heavenly man, so also are those who are of heaven. **⁴⁹ And just as we have borne the image of the earthly man, so shall we bear the image of the heavenly man.**

50 I declare to you, brothers and sisters, that flesh and blood cannot inherit the kingdom of God, nor does the perishable inherit the imperishable. 51 Listen, I tell you a mystery: We will not all sleep, but we will all be changed — 52 in a flash, in the twinkling of an eye, at the last trumpet. For the trumpet will sound, the dead will be raised imperishable, and we will be changed. 53 For the perishable must clothe itself with the imperishable, and the mortal with immortality. **54 When the perishable has been clothed with the imperishable, and the mortal with immortality, then the saying that is written will come true: "Death has been swallowed up in victory."**

55 "Where, O death, is your victory?
Where, O death, is your sting?"

56 The sting of death is sin, and the power of sin is the law. 57 But thanks be to God! He gives us the victory through our Lord Jesus Christ.

58 Therefore, my dear brothers and sisters, stand firm. Let nothing move you. Always give yourselves fully to the work of the Lord, because you know that your labor in the Lord is not in vain.

Based on this passage, I conclude that, since Jesus has been raised from the dead, the following are true for me...if I believe in Him.

My sins are forgiven.
God gives me victory over death through Jesus...eternal
        life.
This victory includes inheriting the kingdom of God.

Once I receive this gift of God based on His grace through faith in Jesus, what is next? Do I just declare victory and continue going about my daily business?

It's not quite that simple.

Justification and Sanctification

There are several excellent passages to look at regarding this question. However, we have been using the Gospel of John, so let's continue in that book. Returning to Jesus' high priestly prayer in John 17 we find the following.

> 13 "I am coming to you now, but I say these things while I am still in the world, so that they may have the full measure of my joy within them. 14 I have given them your word and the world has hated them, for they are not of the world any more than I am of the world. 15 My prayer is not that you take them out of the world but that you protect them from the evil one. 16 They are not of the world, even as I am not of it. 17 **Sanctify them by the truth; your word is truth.** 18 As you sent me into the world, I have sent them into the world. 19 For them I sanctify myself, that they too may be truly sanctified.

I really need to understand the terms *justification* and *sanctification* as they apply to God's work in my salvation. Again I recommend Paul's writing in Romans Chapters 1 through 7 for study on these topics.

- Basically, justification is the act of God of declaring me, an unrighteous sinful man, as righteous (without sin) before Him based on Jesus' righteousness imputed to me through His crucifixion.

- Sanctification is a process done through the work of the Holy Spirit to make me more like Christ.

Also see the work of Wayne Grudem, *Systematic Theology*, (referenced in the appendix) for a full explanation of these critical concepts.

The conclusion of this question for me is salvation is not "one and done." It includes a process of becoming more like Christ (more holy) through God working in my life and through my study, worship, prayer and communion with other Christians. Paul writes about my responsibility in Colossians 3: 1 – 17. Also, see Hebrews 12: 1 – 13.

Finally, I strongly recommend a thorough study of Romans Chapter 3 for an explanation of our sinfulness. And for Paul's wonderful connection of faith and grace to salvation, I recommend Romans Chapter 4 and Ephesians Chapter 2.

Now, let's conclude this work by taking another look at the primary question: What do I believe about Him?

Chapter 5
Conclusion

In this chapter, I want to reexamine our primary question in three different ways. First, we will examine our question through the "eyes" of the blind man Jesus healed. Second, we will look at the famous writings of C.S. Lewis. Finally, we will look at the response of a famous musician who was asked about this issue.

Jesus Healing the Blind Man

The account of Jesus healing the blind man is given in John Chapter 9. It is instructive to read the entire chapter.

> As he went along, he saw a man blind from birth. ² His disciples asked him, "Rabbi, who sinned, this man or his parents, that he was born blind?"
>
> ³ "Neither this man nor his parents sinned," said Jesus, "but this happened so that the works of God might be displayed in him. ⁴ As long as it is day, we must do the works of him who sent me. Night is coming, when no one can work. ⁵ While I am in the world, I am the light of the world."
>
> ⁶ After saying this, he spit on the ground, made some mud with the saliva, and put it on the man's eyes. ⁷ "Go," he told him, "wash in the Pool of Siloam" (this word means "Sent"). So the man went and washed, and came home seeing.
>
> ⁸ His neighbors and those who had formerly seen him begging asked, "Isn't this the same man who used to sit and beg?" ⁹ Some claimed that he was.
>
> Others said, "No, he only looks like him."
>
> But he himself insisted, "I am the man."

¹⁰ "How then were your eyes opened?" they asked.

¹¹ He replied, "The man they call Jesus made some mud and put it on my eyes. He told me to go to Siloam and wash. So I went and washed, and then I could see."

¹² "Where is this man?" they asked him.

"I don't know," he said.

¹³ They brought to the Pharisees the man who had been blind. ¹⁴ Now the day on which Jesus had made the mud and opened the man's eyes was a Sabbath. ¹⁵ Therefore the Pharisees also asked him how he had received his sight. "He put mud on my eyes," the man replied, "and I washed, and now I see."

¹⁶ Some of the Pharisees said, "This man is not from God, for he does not keep the Sabbath."

But others asked, "How can a sinner perform such signs?" So they were divided.

¹⁷ Then they turned again to the blind man, "What have you to say about him? It was your eyes he opened."

The man replied, "He is a prophet."

¹⁸ They still did not believe that he had been blind and had received his sight until they sent for the man's parents. ¹⁹ "Is this your son?" they asked. "Is this the one you say was born blind? How is it that now he can see?"

²⁰ "We know he is our son," the parents answered, "and we know he was born blind. ²¹ But how he can see now, or who opened his eyes, we don't know. Ask him. He is of age; he will speak for himself." ²² His parents said this because they were afraid of the Jewish leaders, who already had decided that anyone who acknowledged that Jesus was the Messiah would be put out of the synagogue. ²³ That was why his parents said, "He is of age; ask him."

24 A second time they summoned the man who had been blind. "Give glory to God by telling the truth," they said. "We know this man is a sinner."

25 He replied, "Whether he is a sinner or not, I don't know. One thing I do know. I was blind but now I see!"

26 Then they asked him, "What did he do to you? How did he open your eyes?"

27 He answered, "I have told you already and you did not listen. Why do you want to hear it again? Do you want to become his disciples too?"

28 Then they hurled insults at him and said, "You are this fellow's disciple! We are disciples of Moses! 29 We know that God spoke to Moses, but as for this fellow, we don't even know where he comes from."

30 **The man answered, "Now that is remarkable! You don't know where he comes from, yet he opened my eyes. 31 We know that God does not listen to sinners. He listens to the godly person who does his will. 32 Nobody has ever heard of opening the eyes of a man born blind. 33 If this man were not from God, he could do nothing."**

34 To this they replied, "You were steeped in sin at birth; how dare you lecture us!" And they threw him out.

35 Jesus heard that they had thrown him out, and when he found him, he said, "Do you believe in the Son of Man?"

36 "Who is he, sir?" the man asked. "Tell me so that I may believe in him."

37 Jesus said, "You have now seen him; in fact, he is the one speaking with you."

38 Then the man said, "Lord, I believe," and he worshiped him.

³⁹ Jesus said, "For judgment I have come into this world, so that the blind will see and those who see will become blind."

⁴⁰ Some Pharisees who were with him heard him say this and asked, "What? Are we blind too?"

⁴¹ Jesus said, "If you were blind, you would not be guilty of sin; but now that you claim you can see, your guilt remains.

This text contains a number of powerful sermons but we will look at just a few critical points.

The religious leaders (Pharisees) were concerned about the fact that this healing took place on the Sabbath. Some thought that Jesus was a sinner since He healed the man on the Sabbath. Some were concerned that this healing coupled with other miracles would lead the people away from "their religion" (Mosaic Law). So they investigated this matter thoroughly by repeated questioning of the man who was healed.

Now let's look at the progression of the blind man's responses.

When first asked how this happened, the blind man responded that **"the man they call Jesus"** had healed him. The emphasis here is on "the man." At this point the blind man refers to Jesus as a man. The second time he is quizzed by the Pharisees he responds differently...this time **He is a prophet** according to the blind man. In the third exchange with the religious leaders, the blind man refers to Him as **a man from God.**

During this exchange the blind man becomes progressively assertive with these religious leaders (even though he is not a learned man...blind from birth...no formal training/schooling). He is not intimidated by the Pharisees. The result is that he is thrown out of the synagogue...he is banned from the only accepted religious organization he knows. This is a crushing result for him. But...Jesus heard that he was thrown out and found him and basically presented the Gospel (Himself) to the blind man. The result is the blind man's fourth and final declaration: **"Lord, I believe, and he worshiped him."**

The blind man started off with the belief that Jesus was a man who could perform miracles. Then, his belief progressed (in faith) so that he declared that Jesus was the Son of God...and he began to worship Him. Can we relate to that kind of progression (growth)?

C. S. Lewis from *Mere Christianity*
C.S. Lewis was one of the most influential Christian writers of his time and perhaps of all time...excluding the apostles. Born in 1898, he had a distinguished teaching and writing career as a professor at Oxford and Cambridge. He authored more than 30 books by the time of his death in 1963. *Mere Christianity* is one of his most distinguished and popular works.

Lewis addresses our basic question regarding who Jesus is on page 52 in a paragraph which has come to be known as, "Liar, Lunatic or Lord." The following is from this chapter in his work.

> I am trying here to prevent anyone saying the really foolish thing that people often say about Him: 'I'm ready to accept Jesus as a great moral teacher, but I don't accept His claim to be God.' That is the one thing we must not say. A man who said the sort of

things Jesus said would not be a great moral teacher. He would either be a lunatic — on a level with the man who says he is a poached egg — or else he would be the Devil of Hell. You must make your choice. **Either this man was, and is, the Son of God: or else a madman or something worse. You can shut Him up for a fool, you can spit at Him and kill Him as a demon; or you can fall at His feet and call Him Lord and God. But let us not come with any patronizing nonsense about His being a great human teacher. He has not left that open to us. He did not intend to.** (*Mere Christianity*, HarperCollins 1980, page 52).

Lewis convincingly argues that Jesus Christ was either a liar, a lunatic (or something worse) or He is the Son of God and Lord!

Now let's look at the response to the same question from the secular perspective of Lewis' fellow countryman, Bono of U2.

Bono of U2
A few days after the Madrid terrorist bombing in 2004, Bono did another in a series of interviews with a French journalist named Michka Assayas. The subject of religion came up regarding terrorism. Bono began to discuss Karma and Grace. He indicated that he believed that, "Jesus took my sins onto the Cross, because I know who I am, and I hope I don't have to depend on my own religiosity."

When Bono said, "It's not our own good works that get us through the gates of heaven," the journalist replied as follows.

That's a great idea, no denying it. Such great hope is wonderful, even though it's close to lunacy, in my view. Christ has his rank among the world's great thinkers. But Son of God, isn't that farfetched?

Bono's answer is basically a modern day version of the position that C. S. Lewis takes on this question. Bono gave the following response.

No, it's not farfetched to me. Look, the secular response to the Christ story always goes like this: he was a great prophet, obviously a very interesting guy, had a lot to say along the lines of other great prophets, be they Elijah, Muhammad, Buddha, or Confucius.
But actually Christ doesn't allow you that. He doesn't let you off that hook.
Christ says:
No. I'm not saying I'm a teacher, don't call me teacher. I'm not saying I'm a prophet. I'm saying: 'I'm the Messiah.' I'm saying: 'I am God incarnate.'

And people say: 'No, no, please, just be a prophet. A prophet, we can take. You're a bit eccentric. We've had John the Baptist eating locusts and wild honey, we can handle that. But don't mention the *M* word! Because, you know, we're gonna have to crucify you.'

And he [Christ] goes:
No, no. I know you're expecting me to come back with an army, and set you free from these creeps, but actually I am the Messiah.

At this point, everyone starts staring at their shoes, and says, 'Oh, my God, he's gonna keep saying this.'

So what you're left with is: either Christ was who He said He was, the Messiah, or a complete nutcase. I mean, we're talking nutcase on the level of Charles Manson. . . . I'm not joking here. The idea that the entire course of civilization for over half of the globe could have its fate changed and turned upside-down by a nutcase, for me, that's farfetched.

Above quotes are from Bono in Conversation with Michka Assayas; Riverhead Books, 2005; page 227).

What conclusions can you draw?

In this chapter, I have presented three views on the primary question *What do I believe about Him?* The blind man went through a progression of thought and belief about Jesus and arrived at the position that He is the Son of God and Lord of all.

C.S. Lewis narrows the question to liar, lunatic, or Lord.

Bono basically agrees with Lewis and gives us a more modern day version of Lewis' position.

So for 90 pages, we have considered the question *What I think about Him?* And for all the reasons stated, I believe that question is very important. But, I must temper that position with the words of C. S. Lewis. The following quote is taken from *The Weight of Glory* by C. S. Lewis in a sermon he originally preached in the Church of Saint Mary the Virgin, Oxford, on June 8, 1942.

I read in a periodical the other day that the fundamental thing is how we think of God.

By God Himself, it is not [*the fundamental thing*]! How God thinks of us is not only more important, but infinitely more important. Indeed, how we think of Him is of no importance **_except in so far as it is related to how He thinks of us_**.

God loves us so much that He sent His only Son to save us from our sins. So, how we think about Jesus is fundamental to how God thinks about us. For that reason, it is critical that we focus on the question posed in this work.

I have answered the question for myself. I have dismissed all other alternatives and I firmly believe the conclusion that Jesus Christ is the only Son of God. I believe that He became a man through the virgin birth, lived on the earth, was crucified and rose from the dead.

That is my position. But who do you say He is?

If you have not come to a conclusion on this question, I hope this work will help you through that process. If you have reached a conclusion, I hope that you will compare your position to what is presented here. In either case, please think long and hard about this fundamental life-changing question!

What About Him?

What About Him
Book Resources

The Bible (NIV is quoted from in the document)

Arthur, Kay *Lord, Only You Can Change Me*, Colorado Springs, CO: WaterBrook Press, 2000

Assayas, Michka, *Bono in conversation with Michka Assayas,* New York, NY: Riverhead Books, 2005

Boice, James Montgomery, *Christ's Call to Discipleship,* Grand Rapids MI: Kregel Publishers, 2013

Boice, James Montgomery,   *John, Volumes 1 – 5*, Grand Rapids MI: Baker Books, 2005

Boice, James Montgomery, *Living by the Book,* Grand Rapids MI: Baker Books, 2000

Boice, James Montgomery, *Renewing Your Mind in a Mindless World,* Grand Rapids MI: Kregel Publishers, 1993

Boice, James Montgomery, *Romans, Volumes 1 – 4,* Grand Rapids MI: Baker Books, 1995

Boice, James Montgomery, *The Parables of Jesus*, Chicago IL: Moody Publishers, 1983

Boice, James Montgomery, *To the Glory of God,* Grand Rapids MI: Baker Books, 2010

Boice, James Montgomery, *Whatever Happened to the Gospel of Grace,* Wheaton IL: Crossway, 2001

Bridges, Jerry, *The Pursuit of Holiness,* Colorado Springs, CO: NavPress, 2006

Bridges, Jerry, *Transforming Grace,* Colorado Springs, CO: NavPress, 2008

Calvin, John, *Institutes of the Christian Religion,* Carlisle, PA: The Banner of Truth, 2014

Calvin, John, *Calvin's Commentaries,* Grand Rapids MI: Baker Books, 2009 (23 volume set)

Carson, D.A., *The Difficult Doctrine of the Love of God,* Wheaton IL: Crossway, 2000

Chalmers, Thomas, *The Explusive Power of a New Affection,* New York: Robert Carter, 1848

Chanty, Walter J., *The Shadow of the Cross,* Carlisle, PA: The Banner of Truth, 1981

Chanty, Walter J., *Today's Gospel,* Carlisle, PA: The Banner of Truth, 1970

DeYoung, Kevin, *Just Do Something,* Chicago IL: Moody Publishers, 2009

Edwards, Jonathan, *Pursuing Holiness in the Lord,* Phillipsburg, NJ: The Jonathan Edwards Institute, 2005

Edwards, Jonathan, *Religious Affections,* Vancouver, British Columbia: Regent College Publishing, 1984

Edwards, Jonathan, *Sermons of Jonathan Edwards,* Peabody, MA: Hendrickson Publishers, Inc., 2005

Edwards, Jonathan, *Sinners in the hands of an Angry God,* Boston, MA: Kneeland and Green, 1741

Greear, J. D., *Stop Asking Jesus Into Your Heart,* Nashville, TN: B&H Publishing Group, 2013

Grudem, Wayne, *Systematic Theology,* Grand Rapids MI: Zondervan, 1994

Hendricks, Howard G. and William D., *Living by the Book,* Chicago IL: Moody Publishers, 2007

Hybels, Bill, *Courageous Leadership,* Grand Rapids MI: Zondervan, 2009

Keller, Timothy, *Counterfeit Gods,* New York, NY: Penguin Group, 2009

Keller, Timothy, *Judges for You,* USA: thegoodbook Co, 2013

Keller, Timothy, *Prodigal God,* New York, NY: Penguin Group, 2008

Kendall, R. T., *The Sermon on the Mount,* Minneapolis MN: Baker, 2011

Lewis, C. S., *Mere Christianity,* San Francisco CA: HarperCollins, 2001

Lloyd-Jones, D. Martyn, *2 Peter,* Carlisle, PA: The Banner of Truth, 1983

Lloyd-Jones, D. Martyn, *Joy Unspeakable,* OK: David C. Cook,1994

Lloyd-Jones, D. Martyn, *Spiritual Depression*, Grand Rapids, MI: William B. Eerdmans Publishing Co., 1965

Lloyd-Jones, D. Martyn, *Studies in the Sermon on the Mount*, Grand Rapids, MI: William B. Eerdmans Publishing Co., 1976

Lloyd-Jones, D. Martyn, *The Cross*, Wheaton IL: Crossway, 1986

MacArthur, John, *1 – 3 John*, Chicago IL: Moody Publishers, 2007

MacArthur, John, *The Gospel According to the Apostles,* Nashville, TN: Thomas Nelson,2000

MacArthur, John, *The Gospel According to the Jesus,* Grand Rapids MI: Zondervan, 2008

MacArthur, John, *The Jesus Answer Book,* Nashville, TN: Thomas Nelson, 2014

MacArthur, John, *The Truth About Grace,* Nashville, TN: Thomas Nelson, 2012

MacArthur, John, *Twelve Ordinary Men*, Nashville, TN: Thomas Nelson, 2002

MaHaney, C. J., *Humility: True Greatness,* Colorado Springs, CO: Multnomah Books, 2005

Manz, Charles C., *The Leadership Wisdom of Jesus,* San Francisco, CA: Berrett-Kohler, 2008

Miller, C. John, *Repentance: A Daring Call to Surrender,* Fort Washington, PA: CLC Publishers, 2009

Morgan, Robert J., *Then Sings My Soul,* Nashville, TN: Thomas Nelson, 2003

Morris, Leon, *Jesus is the Christ,* Grand Rapids, MI: William B. Eerdmans Publishing Company, 1989

Morris, Leon, *The Gospel According to John,* Grand Rapids, MI: William B. Eerdmans Publishing Company, 1995

Morris, Leon, *Revelation,* Grand Rapids, MI: William B. Eerdmans Publishing Company, 1987

North, Brownlow, *The Prodigal Son*, London: Silver Trumpet Publishers, Ltd., 1989

North, Brownlow, *The Rich Man and Lazarus*, London: The Banner of Truth, 1968

Owen, John, *The Mortification of Sin,* USA: Create Space, 2013

Tozer, A. W., *The Pursuit of God*, Ventura, CA: Regal, 2013

Tripp, Paul David, *Forever,* Grand Rapids MI: Zondervan, 2011

Spurgeon, Charles Haddon, *All of Grace,* Shippensburg, PA: Destiny Image, 2007

Stedman, Ray C., *Authentic Christianity*, Grand Rapids, MI: Discovery House, 1996

Stott, John R. W., *Confess Your Sins*, Waco, TX: Word Books, 1974

Stott, John R. W., *The Message of the Sermon on the Mount*, Downers Grove, IL: Inter Varsity Press1978

Piper, John, *A Peculiar Glory,* Wheaton, IL: Inter Varsity Press, 2016

Piper, John, *Don't Waste your Life,* Wheaton IL: Crossway, 2009

Piper, John, *Future Grace*, Colorado Springs, CO: Multnomah Books, 1995

Piper, John, *God is the Gospel,* Wheaton IL: Crossway, 2005

Piper, John, *Life as a Vapor,* Colorado Springs, CO: Multnomah Books, 2004

Piper, John, *The Passion of Jesus Christ,* Wheaton IL: Crossway, 2004

Platt, David, *Radical,* Colorado Springs, CO: Multnomah Books, 2010

Willard, Dallas, *Renewing the Christian Mind,* New York, NY: HarperCollins Publishers, 2016

Also by Harry Carter

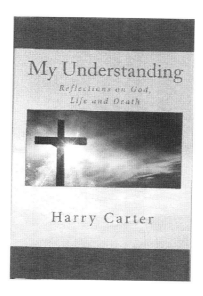

My Understanding is a study of Biblical principles reflected in the Old and New Testaments. The author shares his exploration of what the Bible says about God and Jesus Christ and offers ten conclusions he believes reflect the basic message of God's love and our salvation. His concluding chapter *How then should I live?* reveals the answers he has developed during his spiritual journey. Any Christian seeking a closer relationship with God will find this work a thought-provoking study.

About the Author

Harry S. Carter is an educator, college professor, former college provost and interim college president who has spent much of his career synthesizing complex information into fundamental principles. In recent years, he has turned his inquiries to matters of faith, reading Christian literature extensively to supplement his study of the Holy Bible.

Harry and his wife, Brenda, live in Charleston, S.C. where they are members of First Baptist Church.